1 June 1960
BS

Panther (Josie Billie).

SMITHSONIAN INSTITUTION

BUREAU OF AMERICAN ETHNOLOGY

BULLETIN 161

SEMINOLE MUSIC

By

FRANCES DENSMORE

UNITED STATES

GOVERNMENT PRINTING OFFICE

WASHINGTON : 1956

For sale by the Superintendent of Documents, U. S. Government Printing Office
Washington 25, D. C. - Price $1 (paper cover)

LETTER OF TRANSMITTAL

SMITHSONIAN INSTITUTION,
BUREAU OF AMERICAN ETHNOLOGY,
Washington, D. C., March 30, 1955.

SIR: I have the honor to transmit herewith a manuscript entitled "Seminole Music," by Frances Densmore, and to recommend that it be published as a bulletin of the Bureau of American Ethnology.

Very respectfully yours,

M. W. STIRLING, *Director.*

DR. LEONARD CARMICHAEL,
Secretary, Smithsonian Institution.

FOREWORD

The Seminole of Florida are a Muskhogean tribe originally made up of immigrants who moved down into Florida from the Lower Creek towns on the Chattahoochee River. Their tribal name is derived from a Creek word meaning "separatist" or "runaway," suggesting that they lack the permanent background of the tribes whose music had previously been studied.[1]

The writer's first trip to the Seminole in Florida was in January 1931, and the Indians observed were from the Big Cypress Swamp group. The second visit, begun in November 1931, continued until March of the following year, the study including both the Cypress Swamp and Cow Creek groups of the tribe. Two exhibition villages near Miami afforded an opportunity to see the native manner of life. These were Musa Isle and Coppinger's Tropical Gardens. The managers of both villages extended their cooperation, and the principal interpreter was Cory Osceola, a grandson of the celebrated chief Robert Osceola. Many songs were recorded, and the work was extended to the Seminole in the vicinity of Dania and to the camps of Seminole along Tamiami Trail, especially the camp of Chestnut Billie and that known as Fifteen Mile Camp. In February 1932, a trip was made to the interior of the Big Cypress Swamp under the escort of W. Stanley Hanson, of Fort Myers; five camps were visited and photographed. Continuing her journey, the writer went to the "Indian Prairie" northwest of Lake Okeechobee and thence south into the cabbage palm country, which is the home of the Cow Creek group. Several camps were visited, and the songs were recorded at Brighton through the courtesy of Mrs. Eliza Fielden, the storekeeper. The return to Miami was by way of Fort Lauderdale, where an ancient Seminole burial ground was photographed.

A third trip to the Seminole was made in February 1933, in connection with a survey of Indian music in the Gulf States made possible by a grant-in-aid from the National Research Council. Another visit was made to the Cow Creek group, and songs were again recorded at Brighton.

The only tribal gatherings of the Seminole are the Corn Dance in June and the Hunting Dance in September. The customs of these gatherings differ in the two groups. The songs of the Cypress Swamp

---

[1] See Authorities Cited (Densmore 1910, 1913, 1918, 1922, 1923, 1926, 1929 b, 1929 c, 1932 a, 1932 b, 1936, 1938, 1939, 1942, 1943 a. 1943 b).

group were recorded by Charlie Billie, who is the leader, and by
Panther, who is prominent in the ceremony, while the songs of the
Cow Greek group were recorded by Billie Stewart, who is the leader
in that group. The total number of Seminole songs presented is 243,
including the songs of 28 social dances, songs for success in hunting
and in the ball game, songs used in the treatment of the sick, and
songs connected with legends. Numerous specimens were collected,
including a woman's costume and three canoe models showing the
types of canoes used by the Seminole.

On the second and third trips the writer had the helpful companion-
ship of her sister, Margaret Densmore.

To the National Research Council and to all who assisted in col-
lecting this material the writer extends her appreciation and thanks.

This report closes in 1933, as stated, and does not refer to later
authorities on the Seminole, nor to the recording of additional
Seminole songs by the writer in 1954, under the auspices of the
University of Florida.

CONTENTS

CONTENTS IX

ILLUSTRATIONS*

PLATES

(All plates except frontispiece follow page 218.)

TEXT FIGURE

*The portraits were by Claude C. Matlack, of Miami Beach, Fla.; all except the portrait of Charles Billie (pl. 4, *a*) were taken for the present work. Other illustrations, with a few exceptions, were taken by the author.

LIST OF SONGS

1. ARRANGED IN ORDER OF SERIAL NUMBERS

SONGS WITH HUNTING DANCE—COW CREEK GROUP

SONGS WITH HUNTING DANCE—CALUSA

SONGS OF PRINCIPAL SOCIAL DANCES WITH CORN DANCE—CYPRESS SWAMP GROUP

SONGS OF PRINCIPAL SOCIAL DANCES WITH CORN DANCE—COW CREEK GROUP

2. ARRANGED IN ORDER OF CATALOG NUMBERS

Catalog No.	Title of song	Name of singer	Serial No.	Page
2064	Calusa Corn Dance song	Billie Stewart	25	61
2065	Calusa Hunting Dance song (a)	___do	57	82
2066	Calusa Hunting Dance song (b)	___do	58	82
2067	Calusa Hunting Dance song (c)	___do	59	83
2068	Calusa Hunting Dance song (d)	___do	60	83
2069	Calusa Hunting Dance song (e)	___do	61	84
2070	Calusa Hunting Dance song (f)	___do	62	84
2071	Calusa Hunting Dance song (g)	___do	63	84
2072	Hunting Dance song (a)	Charlie Billie	26	67
2073	Hunting Dance song (b)	___do	27	67
2074	Hunting Dance song (c)	___do	28	68
2075	Hunting Dance song (d)	___do	29	68
2076	Hunting Dance song (e)	___do	30	69

Cata-log No.	Title of song	Name of singer	Serial No.	Page
2077	Hunting Dance song (f)	Charlie Billie	31	69
2078	Hunting Dance song (g)	do	32	69
2079	Hunting Dance song (h)	do	33	70
2080	Buffalo Dance song (a)	Panther	1	43
2081	Buffalo Dance song (b)	do	2	43
2082	Buffalo Dance song (c)	do	3	44
2083	Buffalo Dance song (d)	do	4	44
2084	Corn Dance song (a)	do	5	45
2085	Corn Dance song (b)	do	6	46
2086	Corn Dance song (c)	do	7	47
2087	Corn Dance song (d)	do	8	48
2088	Corn Dance song (e)	do	9	49
2089	Corn Dance song (f)	do	10	50
2090	Corn Dance song (g)	do	11	51
2091	Corn Dance song (h)	do	12	52
2092	Bird Dance song (a)	do	78	98
2093	Bird Dance song (b)	do	79	98
2094	Bird Dance song (c)	do	80	99
2095	Bird Dance song (d)	do	81	100
2096	Bird Dance song (e)	do	82	101
2097	Bird Dance song (f)	do	83	101
2098	Bird Dance song (g)	do	84	101
2099	Bird Dance song (h)	do	85	102
2100	Bird Dance song (i)	do	86	102
2101	Bird Dance song (j)	do	87	103
2102	Bird Dance song (k)	do	88	103
2103	Bird Dance song (l)	do	89	103
2104	Bird Dance song (m)	do	90	104
2105	Bird Dance song (n)	do	91	104
2106	Turkey Dance song	do	132	122
2107	Screech Owl Dance song (a)	do	141	126
2108	Screech Owl Dance song (b)	do	142	126
2109	Screech Owl Dance song (c)	do	143	127
2110	Song for success in hunting (a)	do	208	176
2111	"It moves about as it feeds"	do	209	177
2112	Song for success in hunting (b)	do	210	178
2113	"They are feeding"	do	211	178
2114	"The old bear makes a noise"	do	212	179
2115	The unsuccessful hunter	do	213	179
2116	"We are going to hunt"	do	214	180
2117	A man drives in the game (a)	do		181
2118	"The scaffold is empty" (b)	do		182
2119	"We are tying up the dead animal"	do	215	183
2110	"We search for fat game"	do	216	183
2121	"Feeding the fire"	do	217	184
2122	Alligator Dance song (a)	do	64	92
2123	Alligator Dance song (b)	do	65	92
2124	Closing song of Alligator dance	do	66	93
2125	Snake Dance song (a)	do	188	146

Catalog No.	Title of song	Name of singer	Serial No.	Page
2126	Snake Dance song (b)	Panther	189	146
2127	Catfish Dance song (a)	do	127	120
2128	Catfish Dance song (b)	do	128	120
2129	Catfish Dance song (c)	do	129	121
2130	Catfish Dance song (d)	do	130	121
2131	Quail Dance song (a)	do	122	117
2132	Switchgrass Dance song (a)	do	151	130
2133	Switchgrass Dance song (b)	do	152	131
2134	Switchgrass Dance song (c)	do	153	131
2135	Switchgrass Dance song (d)	do	154	131
2136	Switchgrass Dance song (e)	do	155	131
2137	Switchgrass Dance song (f)	do	156	132
2138	The rabbit brings back a snake	do	231	195
2139	The opossum calls her lost baby	do	229	194
2140	The opossum dies	do	230	194
2141	Song of friendship (a)	do	240	206
2142	Song of friendship (b)	do	241	207
2143	Song of friendship (c)	do	242	207
2144	Song of friendship (d)	do	243	207
2145	Sandhill Crane Dance song (a)	do	137	124
2146	Sandhill Crane Dance song (b)	do	138	124
2147	Sandhill Crane Dance song (c)	do	139	125
2148	Sandhill Crane Dance song (d)	do	140	125
2149	Hunting Dance song (a)	Billie Stewart	34	71
2150	Hunting Dance song (b)	do	35	72
2151	Hunting Dance song (c)	do	36	72
2152	Hunting Dance song (d)	do	37	73
2153	Hunting Dance song (e)	do	38	73
2154	Hunting Dance song (f)	do	39	73
2155	Hunting Dance song (g)	do	40	74
2156	Hunting Dance song (h)	do	41	74
2157	Hunting Dance song (i)	do	42	74
2158	Hunting Dance song (j)	do	43	75
2159	Hunting Dance song (k)	do	44	75
2160	Hunting Dance song (l)	do	45	76
2161	Hunting Dance song (m)	do	46	76
2162	Hunting Dance song (n)	do	47	77
2163	Hunting Dance song (o)	do	48	77
2164	Hunting Dance song (p)	do	49	78
2165	Hunting Dance song (q)	do	50	78
2166	Hunting Dance song (r)	do	51	78
2167	Hunting Dance song (s)	do	52	79
2168	Hunting Dance song (t)	do	53	79
2169	Hunting Dance song (u)	do	54	80
2170	Hunting Dance song (v)	do	55	80
2171	Hunting Dance song (w)	do	56	81
2172	Song of Medicine Men's Dance (a)	do	15	54
2173	Song of Medicine Men's Dance (b)	do	16	55
2174	Song of Medicine Men's Dance (c)	do	17	55

Catalog No.	Title of song	Name of singer	Serial No.	Page
2175	Song of Medicine Men's Dance (d)	Billie Stewart	18	56
2176	Song of an old Dance (a)	----do	178	141
2177	Song of an old Dance (b)	----do	179	142
2178	Song of an old Dance (c)	----do	180	143
2179	Song of an old Dance (d)	----do	181	143
2180	Corn Dance song (i)	----do	19	56
2181	Corn Dance song (j)	----do	20	57
2182	Corn Dance song (k)	----do	21	57
2183	Corn Dance song (l)	----do	22	58
2184	Corn Dance song (m)	----do	23	58
2185	Corn Dance song (n)	----do	24	59
2186	Buzzard Dance song (a)	----do	125	119
2187	Buzzard Dance song (b)	----do	126	119
2188	Chicken Dance song (a)	----do	92	105
2189	Chicken Dance song (b)	----do	93	105
2190	Chicken Dance song (c)	----do	94	105
2191	Chicken Dance song (d)	----do	95	106
2273	Song used in treatment of lumbago	Susie Tiger	203	170
2274	"The white sun-lady"	----do	206	173
2275	Song for the dying	----do	207	174
2276	Song for bringing a child into the world.	----do	205	172
2277	Song for a sick baby	----do	204	171
2278	Song concerning the removal of Seminole to Oklahoma (a).	----do	232	201
2279	Song concerning the removal of Seminole to Oklahoma (b).	Billie Stewart	233	202
2280	Ball game song (a)	----do	218	187
2281	Ball game song (b)	----do	219	188
2282	Ball game song (c)	----do	220	188
2283	Ball game song (d)	----do	221	189
2284	Ball game song (e)	----do	222	189
2285	Ball game song (f)	----do	223	190
2293	Ball game song (g)	----do	224	190
2294	Ball game song (h)	----do	225	190
2295	Ball game song (i)	----do	226	191
2296	Ball game song (j)	----do	227	191
2297	Ball game song (k)	----do	228	191
2298	Alligator Dance song (c)	----do	67	94
2299	Alligator Dance song (d)	----do	68	94
2300	Alligator Dance song (e)	----do	69	94
2301	Alligator Dance song (f)	----do	70	95
2302	Alligator Dance song (g)	----do	71	95
2303	Alligator Dance song (h)	----do	72	95
2304	Alligator Dance song (i)	----do	73	95
2305	Steal-partner Dance song (a)	----do	172	138
2306	Steal-partner Dance song (b)	----do	173	139
2307	Steal-partner Dance song (c)	----do	174	139
2308	Steal-partner Dance song (d)	----do	175	140

Catalog No.	Title of song	Name of singer	Serial No.	Page
2309	Steal-partner Dance song (e)	Billie Stewart	176	140
2310	Steal-partner Dance song (f)	do	177	141
2311	Switchgrass Dance song (g)	do	157	132
2312	Switchgrass Dance song (h)	do	158	132
2313	Switchgrass Dance song (i)	do	159	133
2314	Switchgrass Dance song (j)	do	160	133
2315	Switchgrass Dance song (k)	do	161	133
2316	Switchgrass Dance song (l)	do	162	133
2317	Buffalo Dance song (f)	do	14	54
2384	Buffalo Dance song (e)	do	13	53
2385	Fox Dance song (a)	do	146	129
2386	Fox Dance song (b)	do	147	129
2387	Fox Dance song (c)	do	148	129
2388	Fox Dance song (d)	do	149	130
2389	Fox Dance song (e)	do	150	130
2390	Hair Dance song (a)	do	163	134
2391	Hair Dance song (b)	do	164	135
2392	Hair Dance song (c)	do	165	135
2393	Stomp Dance song (a)	do	99	108
2394	Stomp Dance song (b)	do	100	108
2395	Stomp Dance song (c)	do	101	109
2396	Stomp Dance song (d)	do	102	109
2397	Stomp Dance song (e)	do	103	110
2398	Stomp Dance song (f)	do	104	110
2399	Hinata Dance song (a)	do	105	111
2400	Hinata Dance song (b)	do	106	111
2401	Hinata Dance song (c)	do	107	111
2402	Hinata Dance song (d)	do	108	112
2403	Hinata Dance song (e)	do	109	112
2404	Hinata Dance song (f)	do	110	112
2405	Hinata Dance song (g)	do	111	113
2406	Hinata Dance song (h)	do	112	113
2407	Hinata Dance song (i)	do	113	113
2408	Hinata Dance song (j)	do	114	113
2409	Hinata Dance song (k)	do	115	114
2410	Hinata Dance song (l)	do	116	114
2411	Hinata Dance song (m)	do	117	114
2412	Hinata Dance song (n)	do	118	115
2413	Hinata Dance song (o)	do	119	115
2414	Hinata Dance song (p)	do	120	115
2415	Hinata Dance song (q)	do	121	116
2416	Old Man's Dance song (a)	do	182	144
2417	Old Man's Dance song (b)	do	183	144
2418	Old Man's Dance song (c)	do	184	144
2419	Old Man's Dance song (d)	do	185	145
2420	Old Man's Dance song (e)	do	186	145
2421	Old Man's Dance song (f)	do	187	145
2422	Black Grass Dance song (a)	do	96	106
2423	Black Grass Dance song (b)	do	97	107

Cata-log No.	Title of song	Name of singer	Serial No.	Page
2424	Black Grass Dance song (c) _____	Billie Stewart _____	98	107
2425	Whooping Crane Dance song (a) ____	_____do _____	133	123
2426	Whooping Crane Dance song (b) ____	_____dl _____	134	123
2427	Whooping Crane Dance song (c) ____	_____do _____	135	123
2428	Whooping Crane Dance song (d) ___	_____do _____	136	124
2429	Crawfish Dance song (a) _____	_____do _____	190	147
2430	Crawfish Dance song (b) _____	_____do _____	191	147
2431	Crawfish Dance song (c) _____	_____do _____	192	148
2432	Hair Dance song (d) _____	_____do _____	166	136
2433	Hair Dance song (e) _____	_____do _____	167	136
2434	Hair Dance song (f) _____	_____do _____	168	137
2435	Two-direction Dance song (a) _____	_____do _____	169	137
2436	Two-direction Dance song (b) _____	_____do _____	170	137
2437	Two-direction Dance song (c) _____	_____do _____	171	138
2438	Skunk Dance song (a) _____	_____do _____	197	151
2439	Skunk Dance song (b) _____	_____do _____	198	151
2440	Lizard Dance song (a) _____	_____do _____	76	97
2441	Lizard Dance song (b) _____	_____do _____	77	97
2442	Baby Alligator Dance song (a) _____	_____do _____	74	96
2443	Baby Alligator Dance song (b) _____	_____do _____	75	96
2444	Drunken Dance song (a) _____	_____do _____	193	149
2445	Drunken Dance song (b) _____	_____do _____	194	149
2446	Blackbird Dance song _____	_____do _____	124	118
2447	Rabbit Dance song _____	_____do _____	145	128
2448	Screech Owl Dance song _____	_____do _____	144	127
2449	Quail Dance song (b) _____	_____do _____	123	117
2450	"My old slaves" _____	Susie Tiger _____	234	203
2451	Song to a motherless boy _____	_____do _____	235	203
2452	Song to a child _____	_____do _____	236	204
2453	Drinking song (a) _____	_____do _____	237	205
2454	Drinking song (b) _____	_____do _____	238	205
2455	Drinking song (c) _____	_____do _____	239	206
2456	Drunken Dance song (c) _____	Billie Bowlegs _____	195	150
2457	Drunken Dance song (d) _____	_____do _____	196	150
2458	Quail Dance song (duplication of No. 123).	_____do _____	_____	118
2459	Lightning Bug Dance _____	_____do _____	199	152
2460	Little Bug Dance _____	_____do _____	200	152
2461	Little Fish Dance _____	_____do _____	201	153
2462	Catfish Dance (e) _____	_____do _____	131	121
2463	Little Boys' Dance _____	_____do _____	202	153

SPECIAL SIGNS USED IN TRANSCRIPTIONS OF SONGS

A straight line slanting downward, placed after a note, indicates that the tone trailed downward with a *glissando* and *diminuendo*, the ending of the tone being indistinct.

⌐‾‾‾⌐placed above a series of notes indicates that they constitute a rhythmic unit.

Capital letters indicate periods in the melody.

× indicates a sharp inhalation (cf. p. 215).

PHONETICS

Indian names and words are presented as they are commonly pronounced.

The vowels have continental values. The consonants represent the nearest English equivalent except that *c* stands for *ch*, and *h* for the sound of German *ch* in prepalatal position.

tc is pronounced as in watch.
c is pronounced as sh in shall.
s is pronounced as in set.
ai is pronounced as in aisle.
ng is pronounced as in finger.

NAMES OF SINGERS AND NUMBER OF SONGS TRANSCRIBED

Billie Stewart	153
Panther	63
Susie Tiger	12
Charlie Billie	8
Billie Bowlegs	7
Total	243

INFORMANTS AND INTERPRETERS

Cory Osceola (Cypress Swamp group)
Panther (Cypress Swamp group)
William King, a Creek from Oklahoma (Cow Creek group)

INFORMANTS WHO WERE NOT INTERPRETERS

Billie Motlo   Jim Gopher
John Tiger   Charlie Snow
Mrs. John Tiger

Among other informants were Annie Tommy and Maggie Tiger, of Dania, and Chestnut Billie and Charlie Tiger at the former's camp on the Tamiami Trail.

CHARACTERIZATION OF SINGERS AND INFORMANTS

CYPRESS SWAMP GROUP

Panther (pl. 1, frontispiece), commonly known as Josie Billie, was the principal singer and informant in this group. He belongs to the Panther clan and his Seminole name is Katcha Nokofti, meaning Panther. For that reason he asked to be designated as Panther in the present work. He is a leader in the Corn, Hunting, and other dances of the Cypress Swamp Seminole. For 8 years he worked with the medicine men and he understands their practices, but he is not a "full medicine man." He has frequently been asked to take up that way of life but has declined, saying that he "could not spare the time to be a medicine man as he must earn his living." He has also realized the change that is rapidly taking place in the life of his people.

Panther's home is south of Immokalee, but he was staying at Musa Isle Trading Post, near Miami, when this material was collected. Grateful acknowledgment is made of his assistance in 1931 and 1932. He speaks English fluently, and he often acted as interpreter for other Seminole besides recording songs and giving information concerning Seminole customs. Sixty-three of his songs are presented herein, but the recording ended abruptly. He was absent from the room a few moments, and when he returned he stated that opposition to his assisting had arisen among a few Indians and he did not consider it advisable to record any more songs. This we regretted, as he was willing to sing more and to give further information.

Charlie Billie (pl. 4, a), the other singer from the Cypress Swamp group, is older than Panther and adheres more rigidly to the old ways. He is a leader in the Corn and Hunting dances and recorded their songs, with Cory Osceola (pl. 2, b) interpreting. His right hand is useless, owing to an injury for which he refused proper care. He broke his arm above the wrist, and although he consented to have it set at a hospital, he left during the night, discarding the splints and dressings on his arm. Nothing would induce him to go back to the white doctor. It was said that his hand hung by the tendons and that serious results might follow. This was the condition when he recorded his songs in January 1931. He is shown with his family in plate 8, b.

COW CREEK GROUP

Billie Stewart (pl. 5, c)[2] is a leader in the Corn, Hunting, and other dances of the Cow Creek group, and he recorded more than 200 songs. This is the largest number of songs that the writer has obtained from one Indian. All the records were studied, but only 153 were transcribed. As in other series, many songs have the same characteristics and it is not considered necessary to present all, in a general study of the music of a tribe. Billie Stewart recorded about half the songs in 1932 and the remainder a year later, the recording on both trips being done at Brighton. The retentive memory of an Indian singer was shown in a remark made by Stewart when the last of his songs were being recorded. He hummed a melody and said, "I sang that for you a year ago, so I won't sing it again." His Seminole name is Ga'tcayeho'la, the first two syllables meaning "Tiger" and the rest of the word having no meaning.

In appearance and manner of life Billie Stewart does not resemble the Seminole of the Cypress Swamp group. He has never been connected with an "exhibition village," but follows the native manner of life. A visit was made to his home in the cabbage palm region. He is respected by white people in the vicinity, and his use of English is sufficient for ordinary conversation. In his first recording of songs he was assisted by his friend Charlie Snow, who has a better English vocabulary, and his second recording was done with William King as interpreter. In his response to plans for work and in his grasp of the purpose of the present work, Billie Stewart resembled the best type of men in other tribes. He does not know the meaning of the native name Stapah'ki that was given him when a child.

Susie Tiger is the wife of Billie Stewart, and her Seminole name is O'mala'gi, meaning "Let us all go." Her grandparents gave her this name, which was original and not inherited. She was born at the time the Seminole were going to Oklahoma and her grandfather felt that everyone had gone, so she received this name. Susie Tiger treats the sick in the native manner (1933) and she recorded songs that she uses in connection with that treatment. She also recorded songs that are "taught to the children as soon as they are old enough to appreciate them." She speaks even less English than her husband, and it was fortunate that William King could interpret her interesting information.

Billie Bowlegs is a prominent member of the Cow Creek group and a descendant of the famous chief of that name. He lives near Okeechobee City and recorded his songs at Brighton, in 1933.

---

[2] Died 1938. The name "Stewart" is thought to have come down from John Stuart, the last representative of England among the Seminole.

INFORMANTS WHO DID NOT RECORD SONGS

Billie Motlo (pl. 2, a)[3] is one of the oldest members of the Cypress Swamp group and lived at Musa Isle when giving his information in 1931 and 1932. He understood the making of canoes and constructed models of various types (cf. p. 31). His native name is A'tske'ci, which was not translated.

John Tiger contributed further information on canoes and other subjects. His death occurred while the work was in progress. (See "Death and Burial," p. 34.) The wife of John Tiger (pl. 4, b) was the principal informant concerning the clothing and adornments of the Seminole women.

Charlie Snow (pl. 5, b)[4] is a member of the Cow Creek group and a brother of Sampson Snow whose camp in the cabbage palm region was visited. He speaks English brokenly but is particularly well informed and added interesting information to the subjects under discussion with Billie Stewart in 1932 and 1933.

Annie Tommy and Maggie Tiger live in the little village at the United States Government School, near Dania. The latter is commonly known as Missie Tiger. In contrast to the native dwellings of the Seminole, they live in houses erected by the Government. They were much interested in the present work and contributed interesting information on food and manner of life.

Chestnut Billie operates an "exhibition village" on Tamiami Trail (pl. 9, a). Much information concerning native life was obtained in this village on many visits. Charlie Tiger, a relative of Chestnut Billie's, was visiting at the camp on one occasion and added details of interest concerning fishing.

Many other Seminole gave information during the writer's numerous visits to their camps and villages, among them being Tiger Tail and Sam Willie, the latter shown with his son in native costume (pl. 3, a, b).

INTERPRETERS

The first interpreter employed among the Seminole was Cory Osceola (pl. 2, b), a grandson of the celebrated chief Robert Osceola. He interpreted during the recording of songs by Charlie Billie in 1931, and his influence was of great assistance in securing the favor of the Seminole. He also gave information when desired.

Panther, as already stated, spoke English easily and acted as interpreter on numerous occasions when information was desired from members of the Cypress Swamp group.

---

[3] Died 1936.
[4] Died 1936.

William King, a Creek Indian from Wetumka, Hughes County, Okla., has visited the Florida Seminole each year since 1925 in the capacity of a missionary. He and his wife were staying at Billie Stewart's camp when the present work was in progress in 1933, and he consented to act as interpreter. He said that he and the Cow Creek Seminole understood one another but that he could not interpret for members of the Cypress Swamp group. His cooperation made possible the securing of many details concerning old customs and beliefs.

SEMINOLE MUSIC

By Frances Densmore

THE SEMINOLE IN HISTORY [5]

Florida was a Spanish colony long before Jamestown was settled or the Mayflower reached the shore of New England. A map made in 1502 shows Florida, and as early as 1510 the Spanish Council of the Indies claimed that ships of Spain had gone thither. Ponce de Léon received a grant to discover and settle "Bimini" in 1513, this legendary island said to contain the Fountain of Youth. During the Easter season of 1515 he came in sight of Florida and gave it the name "Pascua Florida," from the Spanish name for the season. He believed that he had discovered a large island. Later he returned to settle the land but was wounded in an attack by Indians and died in Cuba. Fernandez de Córdoba, according to some writers, landed on the west coast of Florida in 1517, but was attacked by a large band of Indians and died of his wounds.

About 1528 De Narváez landed on the west coast and took up his residence near the present site of Tallahassee where the natives harassed his little settlement in various ways until a remnant of the expedition went away, finally reaching the Spanish settlements in Mexico.

Ten years later, in 1538, Hernando de Soto set out from Spain with 7 ships and a carefully selected company of 600 men. He was a man of experience, having served as a soldier in the West Indies and accompanied Pizarro in his conquest of the Inca in Peru. He landed near the same spot as Narváez and sent two of his leaders with strong forces into the interior to seek and capture some Indians who could be used as guides. The Indians resisted him stubbornly, but a few captives were taken. De Soto returned hostility and cruelty in like manner, making even greater enemies of the natives. After his death Florida remained for many years in the hands of the Indians.

The military efforts of Spain having failed, the next attempt was made from a religious standpoint. A few priests determined to go to Florida, and they landed in Tampa Bay. The first two priests who landed were promptly put to death. A third landed alone and met the same fate, after which the party went to Cuba.

---

[5] Condensed from "A Short History of Florida" (Leake, 1929).

1

Undaunted by failures, Spain tried another method. King Philip II entrusted the conquest and settlement of Florida to Don Luis de Velasco, Governor of Mexico, who had been successful in dealing with the Indians of that country. In 1559 a carefully planned expedition was sent by him from Veracruz, consisting of 1,500 soldiers and settlers and several priests, carrying enough provisions to last a year. This expedition landed near the present site of Pensacola and made a brave attempt. After its failure King Philip gave up the effort to conquer Florida, though later he tried to colonize it.

Meantime the entire east coast of the continent was claimed for France, and Jean Ribault led an expedition into what is now South Carolina. This failed, and a second attempt was made by the French in 1564. This was received in a friendly manner by the Indians who brought gifts of fruits and vegetables and showed the settlers how to plant corn and catch fish. Unfortunately, the French wasted valuable time in searching for gold and hidden treasure, alienating the friendship of the Indians by harsh treatment. Provisions were low and they decided to return to France but were met by King Philip's colonizing expedition under Don Pedro Menendez de Aviles. This leader had orders to kill all Protestants in the region, and as most of Ribault's men were of that faith they escaped by going out to sea. Menendez killed all the French Protestants except a few musicians and mechanics, built a log fort at St. Augustine, mounted 80 cannon and established the first stronghold of Spain in America. It is said that many Indians accepted the Catholic faith.

The French Government did not avenge this action, but a French soldier, Dominique de Gourges, organized and financed an expedition of 3 ships and 200 men, sailing to Cuba, the Bahamas, St. Augustine, and two similar forts on the St. John's River. The Spanish had made enemies of the Indians, but De Gourgas cultivated their friendship, distributing presents. In the crew of one of his ships was a trumpeter who had been in Florida. The Indians recognized him and greeted his coming with every manifestation of joy. Aided by the Indians under Chief Satourina, this expedition captured all the Spanish forts except St. Augustine. The expedition then returned to France.

Twice before the end of the 17th century St. Augustine suffered from attacks by the English. Sir Francis Drake burned the fort in 1586, and it was plundered in 1665 by Captain Davis, an English freebooter. By a treaty in 1763 Florida was given to England in exchange for Havana, and England then owned all the territory between the Atlantic Ocean and the Mississippi River. Four years later Dr. Andrew Trunbull, a Scotsman and a member of the Governor's council, brought 1,500 colonists from Minorca, Italy, Greece, Smyrna, and other Mediterranean islands and established the settlement known as New Smyrna on Mosquita Inlet.

During the Revolution Florida remained loyal to Great Britain, but in 1779, when Spain declared war against England, the Governor of Louisiana invaded west Florida, and Pensacola was surrendered to Spain. From long experience the Spaniards feared serious trouble with the Indians and began to cultivate their good will. A leader had arisen among the Indians in the person of Alexander McGillivray who was chief of the Creeks and the son of a Scottish trader and a Creek woman. Representing both the Creeks and the Seminole, and acting with great duplicity, he negotiated a treaty between these tribes and Spain by which no white man could cross the territory occupied by the Indians without consent from Spain. There was much trouble over boundaries, and the Indians were badly deceived by William Augustus Bowles, an adventurer from Maryland, who married a daughter of a Creek chief and lived among the Indians for some time.

The Government of the United States tried to persuade Spain to cede Florida before the war of 1812. Seven years later Spain sold Florida to the United States for five million dollars, on condition that the United States assume certain Spanish claims, and Florida was taken over by the United States in July 1821.

General Jackson was the first governor of Florida under the United States. The Indians were far from satisfied with the policy of the United States toward them, as stated by Jackson, and saw that it would be quite different from life under the easy-going Spanish governors at Pensacola and St. Augustine.

Governor Jackson left Florida in 1821 and in the following year William P. Duval was appointed Governor by President Monroe. The Seminole were not pleased with the governmental policy of Monroe and when Governor Duval called a council at Fort Moultrie to make definite plans, a few of the powerful chiefs refused to enter into any negotiations with the white men and said they would be bound by no treaty made by other chiefs. However, the conference continued several days and a treaty was finally signed by which the Indians gave up all claim to lands in Florida except those granted them by the Government. These lands constituted a large reservation 20 miles south of Micanopy and the Indians were promised many benefits as well as a considerable sum of money. Having made this agreement, Governor Duval went among the Indians, trying to make them satisfied with the arrangement and promising them a year in which to prepare for removal, during which time no white settlers were to be allowed on the land. At the end of the year they were not ready and the time was extended.

Enemathla, leader of the Tallahassee and foremost chief among the Indians, was deposed by Governor Duval at a time when he was inciting the Indians to war against the white men. Enemathla made his way into Georgia and joined the Creeks.

The Indians did not like reservation life, white settlers encroached upon them, and gradually the Government began to consider moving all the Indians to west of the Mississippi River.

A treaty was made with some of the Florida chiefs in 1832 by which the Government would send these chiefs, with their agent and interpreter, to examine the land to which it was proposed that the Indians be removed. Although the chiefs said they were satisfied with the land when they saw it, they opposed removal when they returned to Florida. The Seminole had separated themselves from the Creeks and refused to go to any reservation on which they would be obliged to live with the Creeks. The Indians objected to the colder climate and the scarcity of firewood, and it appeared as though they might oppose the plan with force. In 1834, just as the question of removal was becoming acute, Governor Duval died.

General Jackson, Florida's first governor, had then become President, and he appointed John Eaton as Duval's successor. Three governors ruled in Florida during the next 7 years. The Government was still determined to move the Indians west, and the Seminole war was their protest. This was fought from 1836 to 1842 with bitter fighting and intense bad feeling on both sides.

The actual start of the Seminole war was due to Osceola, son of a Creek woman and an Englishman named William Powell who lived among the Creeks. While Osceola was still a child his mother came from Georgia and joined the Seminole, bringing him with her. Osceola grew up among the Seminole, opposed their removal, and used his influence against the Government in every way. He broke up a council between General Thompson, then United States agent, and the Indians by sticking his knife in the table and crying, "This is the only treaty I will ever make with the whites." Later he ambushed and murdered Charlie Emthla, a chief who favored peaceful removal. Immediately afterward the Indians began to buy large quantities of gunpowder. General Thompson noticed this, reported it, and was forbidden to sell more powder to the Indians. Angered by this restriction, Osceola and a band of his followers ambushed and killed General Thompson and Lieutenant Smith, burned the store and Government buildings, killed the employees at the settlers' store, and set out to join their tribe in the Big Wahoo Swamp. The Seminole war had begun.

On the same day on which General Thompson was killed (December 28, 1835) Major Dade and 139 American soldiers were ambushed and killed near the Withlacoochee River. The succession of officers commanding the American troops is apart from our present interest. In the spring of 1837 certain chiefs promised their influence for removal. This was a sham in order to gain time for planting crops, and soon afterward Osceola persuaded the Indians to escape into the Everglades. A few months later he and three other chiefs were captured and imprisoned. Osceola died at Fort Moultrie, but the other chiefs escaped and returned to their people, inciting them to further opposition to the whites.

The last great battle of the Seminole war was fought in December 1837, and the following spring 1,500 Florida Indians were sent to Arkansas. The few Indians remaining in Florida continued the war and constantly raided the settlements. More Indians were removed, and in 1842 General Worth recommended that the few who remained be allowed to do so, peace being made on that basis.

The Seminole war lasted 7 years and cost the lives of 1,400 American soldiers. Our forces in the field at one time numbered 9,000 while the armed strength of the Indians, ambushed and moving through familiar country, was estimated at only 2,000.

The relation of the Creeks to the Seminole has been described as follows: About the year 1750 "a few hundred Creeks of Georgia, becoming dissatisfied with that tribe, left Georgia and wandered south into the swamps and forests of the Florida peninsula. Secoffee was their leader at that time and he led them into the Spanish colony of Florida. From that time they absolutely refused to be represented in the councils of the Creeks. They elected their own rulers and became in all respects a separate tribe. They settled first in the rich country around Alachua" (Winter, 1918, p. 130). These Indians "received the name of Seminoles, or 'Runaways.' The Mickasukies, legitimate owners of the country, at first opposed these migrations, but they were too feeble to make any effective resistance. In a short time all the Indians amalgamated, and joined in efforts to resist the white men—the common enemy of all (Gifford, 1925, p. 20). The Creek form of the tribal name is "*Sim-a-nó-le*, or *Isti simanóle*, 'separatist,' 'runaway'" (Mooney, 1912, pt. 2, p. 500).

THE SEMINOLE OF MODERN TIMES AND THEIR ABODE

A Seminole chief named Wild Cat was living in 1896. Mr. Henry, who was connected with the Musa Isle Trading Post, said that his father came to Florida by wagon at about that time, which preceded the construction of the East Coast Railway. Wild Cat told Mr. Henry's father that the Seminole were descended from giants, 6 or 8 feet tall, who "had always lived here." He said, further, that these giants had ceremonial mounds with square tops. These mounds were places for prayer and were also used as lookouts, 2 to 4 men being stationed there at all times. The grass was burned for a considerable distance around these mounds, and if anyone attempted to cross the burned area he was captured and burned on top of the mound. It was said that mounds had been found near Sarasota on the west coast of Florida but that investigation showed they had been made by white men. Such are the traditions held by the Seminole of today. The Seminole of southern Florida, known as the Cypress Swamp group, resent the idea of relationship with the Creek tribe, saying this is limited to the northern, or the Cow Creek group. Their language does not resemble that of the Creek, which they are unable to understand, while the Seminole of the Cow Creek group understand the Creek language, and a Creek interpreter was employed when some of their songs were recorded. Their abode is chiefly in the cabbage palm region, southwest of Lake Okeechobee.

The present attitude of the Seminole toward the white race is that of aloofness (1931–33). Unlike other tribes, the Seminole retain their native manner of life and hold themselves aloof from interference, although an agency of the Government has recently been established at Dania, with a school that is attended by a few pupils. The Seminole, as a tribe, have kept their old beliefs and protected the authority of the old men. Independent of aid, they have developed a commercial ability which makes them self-supporting, and they have succeeded in doing this with a minimum use of the English language.

The peculiar status of this tribe has been made possible by their retention of the part of Florida known as the Everglades. Until recent years this section has held only a slight attraction for the white men. Hunters and trappers have sought game in its wild places, but the Seminole have been undisputedly in possession. They have hunted the alligator, otter, raccoon, deer, and other animals, selling the hides for enough to satisfy their simple wants. With the proceeds of the hunt they have bought cotton cloth for their clothing, simple utensils for cooking, and such articles of food as they could not obtain from nature. By maintaining the balance between desire and possession they have lived contentedly in the old manner, whether on the hammocks of the Everglades, in the cabbage palm region, or in their villages. They are still under the authority of the old men who live in the depths of the Everglades, rarely, if ever, coming near the abode of the white man.

The part of the Everglades visited in 1931 consisted of wet meadows of "saw grass," dotted with hammocks of various sizes. Spaces of open water were visible in the tall grass. Across these open spaces the Indian poles his dugout or forces it through the grass. The depth of the water varies from a few inches to 3 or 4 feet, and the size of the hammock varies from a few feet to several acres. The hammocks consist of firm ground, slightly above the level of the water, and are densely wooded. In the larger hammocks a camp is entirely hidden from view, and some are large enough to include open ground where

deer may graze. There are trails made by animals when traveling
from one hammock to another, the trails being visible to an observer
in an airplane. The network of these trails forms part of the knowledge of an Indian hunter. A temporary camp may be located in a
small hammock and entirely concealed by the vegetation. A Seminole
family may live in a typical village (pl. 12, *a*) part of the year, or
camp near a little garden where they cultivate corn and other vegetables, but in the hunting season they usually camp where the game
is most abundant or make their camp wherever the occupation of the
time may lead them. The ground plan of a Seminole village as seen
from a dirigible is shown in plate 12, *b*.

Inland water breaks through the barrier surrounding the Florida
peninsula finding its way to the sea. These watercourses are bordered
by dense tropical vegetation, one of the most picturesque being known
as Arch Creek. Such streams are the avenues to the depths of the
Everglades, and on these streams the Seminole travel in their canoes.
Rare beauty of vegetation is seen on these watercourses and mangrove
trees abound in the swamps. The southwestern border of the Everglades, along the ocean, presents a different landscape (pl. 13, *b*). One
of the largest areas is known as Big Cypress Swamp, lying slightly
west of the southern part of the peninsula, and from this area came
the singers and informants of the Cypress Swamp group.

The Seminole refer to themselves as A'jia'tki, which means "white
corn," and say that in the beginning they were white people. A
legend of the origin of the white corn was related by Susie Tiger
(cf. p. 197).

SEMINOLE CAMPS AND VILLAGES

A trip into the Big Cypress Swamp was made on February 8, 1932,
under the escort of W. Stanley Hanson of Fort Myers, Fla., who is
said to be more familiar with the region and the Indians than any
other white man. The trip was made in Mr. Hanson's car, the party
consisting of the writer and her sister Margaret, Mr. and Mrs.
Hanson, and a young Seminole named John Cypress. The localities
visited comprised four camps in the swamp and a camp near the town
of Immokalee.

From Fort Myers to Immokalee there was no recognizable road
through the sand. Mr. Hanson explained that the word "Immokalee"
means "my village." The town consists of only two or three houses,
and the Indian village is across the railroad track. This village, or
camp, consists of five houses in the style of all Seminole dwellings.
The camp is not always occupied by the same families, anyone passing that way being allowed to stay as long as may be convenient. In

this camp, on our arrival, we found Wilson Cypress, to whose brothers the houses in the camp belong. He was making an ox yoke (pl. 10, *a*) and was said to be an expert worker in wood. The family was traveling in a covered wagon, drawn by oxen, and had all their paraphernalia with them. Under the platform of one house the chickens and a pig were roaming, and on the platform of another house a little boy was practicing the writing or printing of English letters, his pencil and paper being near and evidently treasured. An interesting fan was seen and purchased. This fan was made of the wing of the black ibis and was used for general purposes, such as fanning the fire to make it burn. About 500 feet away were three more houses of the same sort, which were unoccupied. This part of the camp was not visited.

Leaving Immokalee, the party traveled to the camp of Charlie Cypress known as New Florida Camp. The term "Big Cypress Swamp" refers to the area of the swamp, not the size of the trees. The entire region is almost impassable in a car in ordinary seasons, but the dry weather had converted it into an expanse of dry grass. It was found that Ocaloacoochee Slough was practically dry. In the region traversed after crossing the Slough there were broad stretches of dry, tall grass, many acres of low palmettos, and a considerable growth of pine. The car was guided skillfully through woods in which there appeared to be no path and no openings between the trees straight enough for a car to proceed.

Arriving at Charlie Cypress' camp, we saw that, as we had been informed, the family had been absent for some time. The usual occupants are Charlie Cypress, his son John, who is unmarried, and his son-in-law Albert Billie, with the latter's family. The camp stands on a hammock which is usually surrounded by water, especially on the side where the houses are located; yet it is not called a "boat village" as the owners use a Model T Ford car which can run through shallow water. The hammock is now surrounded by a grassy meadow and the buildings are invisible from outside, as they are in a thick growth of trees. The diagram of the camp (fig. 1) shows a path 200 or 300 feet long (*k*) leading to the houses. This path is chiefly through tall pines and thick underbrush. No hesitation was felt in entering the camp as John was a member of the party. The diagram shows the relative location of the structures but not their relative size. The camp contains two living houses (*B* and *E*), the former being intended for several persons and the latter, belonging to John Cypress, being for his personal use. The larger house has a floor (platform) made of logs of the cabbage palm tree, split and hand-hewn. The thatch is of the usual material, but the roof has no gable, the house being more nearly square than the Seminole dwellings previously seen. Various

articles were stored in the rafters, including several modern hoes, a
glass jar of seed corn, and a piece of the heart of a cabbage palm, used
for food.

The cooking fire, with logs arranged like spokes of a wheel, is under
a sloping thatch (fig. 1, *C*). Another sloping thatch, also without
sides, extends almost to the ground and is used as a storage shack
(*G*). Two uncovered platforms are in the camp, one on which a
kettle was overturned, showing its use for cooking utensils (*D*) and the
other being used for drying squashes and pumpkins, several remaining
upon it (*H*). At one corner an old garment was hung on a pole to

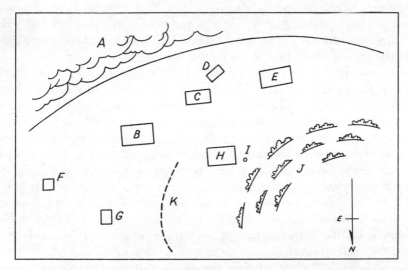

FIGURE 1.—Diagram of New Florida Camp in the Everglades: *A*, Edge of hammock; *B*, principal dwelling; *C*, fire with slanting roof above it; *D*, platform
with inverted kettle; *E*, smaller dwelling belonging to John Cypress; *F*,
waterhole; *G*, storage shack; *H*, platform on which squash were drying; *I*,
pole with garment as "scarecrow"; *J*, garden; *K*, path for entering and
leaving camp. (Relative position is shown but not relative size.)

serve as a scarecrow (*I*). A waterhole is located at *F*, this being a
hole into which the water seeps and from which it is drawn by means
of a pail. The edge of the hammock (*A*) is at the top of a steep bank,
perhaps 3 or 4 feet high, and is marked by trees covered with thick
vines. The garden plot (*J*) was not cleared, but tamps and mallets
for driving stakes were seen. Within the garden were mulberry trees
which had been planted and taro which had been set out. There was
stubble of corn, and wild papaws and pumpkins were seen growing.
Two banana trees were in the garden, these being the coarse variety
sometimes called "horse bananas." Beyond the garden were live oaks,

festooned with trailing moss. As the Seminole are not constantly at home to tend their gardens, they seem to think it safe to have the ground covered by various growths.

The third camp visited was Old Florida Camp, which was abandoned after the death of Frank Charlie's wife about 1927. Both this and New Florida camps were photographed. It is the Seminole custom to leave a camp in which a death has occurred and not occupy it again. After this one was abandoned the camp known as New Florida was built. The old camp contained two thatched houses, a third having fallen down. The floorboards of the houses were burned in spots, showing that the camp had been used by white hunters. The hammock is not so high as that on which New Florida camp is built. Papaws were growing around it and the bright yellow globes of wild oranges were seen in the bushes. A pail had been left at the waterhole, but the atmosphere of the place told of its long solitude.

The fourth camp was Charlie Cypress's hunting camp in which he was living at the time. The structures consisted of a tent without sides, made by stretching a tarpaulin for a roof, a rough structure for living quarters, and a neat thatched structure for cooking. The kettles and pans were stuck on the trees (pl. 10, c). Attention is directed to the vegetation in the background in contrast to that shown with New Florida camp. Mr. and Mrs. Richard Osceola live in this camp, and Mrs. Osceola was mixing biscuits for supper at the cooking table (pl. 10, b). Lena Osceola is about 30 years of age, a daughter of Charlie Cypress, who, in accordance with custom, has brought her husband to live with her parents. A high platform at one side was used for cutting meat, this being especially needed in a hunting camp. "Horse-bananas" grew wild in the fields and two "hands" of them were in the camp, ready for eating. Two sewing machines were in use, and a baby was swinging in a hammock. Tanned deerskins were spread on the ground, giving a pleasing effect of color.

The fifth camp visited was Charlie Dixie's hunting camp, more than halfway from the last-named camps to Immokalee. This could be used by anyone, and it happened that John Cypress's family was there temporarily. This camp contained no platforms and the people slept on the ground, palmettos being spread for the purpose; they also ate on the ground. A "side of meat" was seen hanging up. The small children in this camp wore no clothing. An interesting old woman was seen, sitting on the ground. Her hair was arranged in a knob about 3 inches high, and her beads were loose around her neck. Beside her, at the top of the pole, were two or three dark, circular objects resembling doughnuts, pierced by the pole. On being questioned, she said they were made of deer meat and melted fat and

that she chewed them for food (cf. p. 26).   This camp is located on
flat ground, not far from a road.   An interesting village scene is
shown in plate 13, *a*, and a view in the Everglades in plate 13, *b*.

VILLAGES IN THE CABBAGE PALM REGION

A few days prior to the trip to the Big Cypress Swamp, a visit was
made to several camps in the cabbage palm region, southwest of Lake
Okeechobee.   The purpose of this trip was to arrange for work with
Billie Stewart, the leader of the dances in the Cow Creek group of
Seminole.

On arrival at Brighton, north of the cabbage palm region, a call
was made at the general store where Mrs. Eliza Fielden, wife of the
postmaster and storekeeper, said that Billie Stewart had gone on a
hunting trip.   A message was sent to him by a young Indian who
came into the store with hides for shipment.   As the singer could
not be contacted that afternoon, it was decided to go into the country,
with a possibility of finding Indians in the neighboring camps.   Mrs.
Fielden kindly consented to show the way and the trip was made in
the writer's car.   Grateful acknowledgment is made of her assistance
at this time and during all the subsequent work with the Cow Creek
Seminole.

After traveling a few miles toward the south we turned east, the
road extending along the bank of a dry canal and consisting only of
a trail in the deep white sand that had been thrown up when the ex-
cavation was made for the canal.

Finding that the camps were too far away to visit that evening
the party returned to Brighton.   The next morning a more successful trip was made with Dan Norton, who used his own car.
Mrs. Fielden was again a member of the party.   Traversing the
same road as on the previous day we turned abruptly to the left,
and after crossing a gully we entered a flat plain covered with tall
grass.   A few indistinct trails cross this plain, resembling the paths
on the desert in southern Arizona.   It would have been impossible
for anyone who was not familiar with the country to find his way
but Mr. Norton knew the region, as he had herded cattle through it.

Our first call was at Billie Buster's camp.   Billie Buster is an old
man who lives alone.   When he goes to town he walks beside his
horse, allowing the horse to carry his bundles.   He was recently
offered $8.00 a month by the Government but refused it, saying that
he was able to take care of himself.   His camp was empty when we
called, as he had gone hunting, but he had left the camp in excellent
order.   His fire is the typical "spoke arrangement" of logs, and his
utensils are under a shelter, not on an open platform as in some camps.

His garden is strongly fenced and shows considerable planting, but, according to Seminole custom, the ground was not entirely cleared, nor had it been cultivated (pl. 15, c).

The second camp visited was the hunting camp of Billie Buster and Sampson Snow. Both men were absent on the hunt, the only persons at home being the wife of Sampson Snow and his mother, known as Sallie Micco. The camp was well concealed in the trees and its equipment did not differ from that of other camps which have been described. There is a painstaking care in the details of Seminole housekeeping that is almost pathetic in view of its simplicity. In this camp a hen was sitting on some eggs. The women had put the hen in a box elevated more than 2 feet above the ground, under a tree, and over the box they had arranged a shelter of boughs, making a safe, shady place for the setting hen.

After leaving this camp we went along the edge of the hammock in which it was located and chanced to see a number of hides placed on a tree to dry (pl. 15, a). The sharp projections on the trunk of the cabbage palm are used as hooks, and on these the hunter had hung the hides, stretched on drying frames. This was a favorable place as they were in the sun and air, and were not likely to be disturbed. A small but typical hammock of cabbage palms is seen in the distance of the oblong picture.

After this reconnaissance it was necessary to return to Fort Myers before taking the trip into the Big Cypress Swamp, but it was arranged that Billie Stewart would be at the Brighton store on the morning of February 12, prepared to record songs and give information concerning them. Mrs. Fielden consented to explain the work to him, and there seemed no doubt of his willingness to do what was asked. It was said that he always keeps his word.

On the appointed day, the writer returned to Brighton, Billie Stewart was ready to record, and the work among the Cow Creek Seminole was begun. His first song was a Corn Dance song of the Calusa (No. 25).

FIFTEEN MILE CAMP

About 15 miles west of Miami, on Tamiami Trail, is a camp known as Fifteen Mile Camp. It is said to be owned by William Osceola, but it is occupied by different families from the Everglades as a temporary abode while transacting business in Miami. A visit to this camp was made at the suggestion of Cory Osceola, who gave permission for the use of his name when entering it.

An inquiry at the little store on the Trail brought the information that the camp could be reached by crossing the canal on a little bridge and turning left through the tall grasses, but the storekeeper stated that the ground was wet and the path through the grasses might be impassable. A man from the camp, known as Small-pox Billie, was seen walking along the other bank of the canal carrying a canoe pole on his shoulder. He was going up a side canal and later was seen pushing his canoe into the water. After crossing the little bridge we entered a narrow, winding path through the grasses.

When we entered the camp we realized that we were regarded as intruders. Even the name of Cory Osceola brought no response from the Seminole women who were busy with sewing and other tasks. In the middle of the camp was a cooking fire with the logs in the familiar "spoke" arrangement (pl. 17, b). A piece of fish was drying on the limb of a tree, and kettles were hung on the branches (pl. 10, c). Though these people were moving from place to place they had their supply of coontie ("comptie") flour in bags, on a low platform, covered with palmetto leaves (cf. pl. 18, a). The taking of several photographs was made possible by the usual gifts of money and fresh fruit, but the women and children were entirely unresponsive. They understood English, but made no reply to questions. At last I prepared to leave, saying that I had more oranges in the car, also that I had bought a used car and wished they might see it. Buying a "used car" is a common transaction among the Seminole and this appealed to them at once. The women and children indicated their intention to go back to the car with us, and led the way through the tall grass. On the bank of the canal, before crossing the bridge we met a man and two boys, returning with two hides and a fish.

When we arrived at the other side of the canal, our car received a thorough inspection. The women looked it all over, and discussed it in Seminole. It would have been interesting to know their conclusions as to its value. There were plenty of oranges in the car, which were accepted by the Seminoles with evident pleasure. The camp was then photographed from that side of the canal. The typical vegetation of the Everglades is shown at the right in plate 15, a. The camp, the little bridge, and the canoe appear in plate 15, b; beyond the camp, a number of garments were hung to dry. Such garments usually appear as a bright spot in the background of a Seminole camp. A view of the region is shown in plate 15, c.

CHESTNUT BILLIE'S VILLAGE

An interesting village on Tamiami Trail, about 10 miles from the town of Everglades, is known as Chestnut Billie's village. It is an individual project of this young Seminole and retains the native atmosphere, although it is open to the public. A narrow bridge spans the canal which borders the Trail (pl. 9, a). Chestnut Billie is standing on the bridge. Charles Tiger, an old man, standing in the canoe has brought him poles and four live fish. Crossing this bridge, one enters a tiny curio shop and passes thence, by an abrupt turn, into Chestnut Billie's village, occupied by his relatives. The village is hidden from the Trail by a high fence and surrounded by the heavy vegetation of the Everglades. The clearing had been made recently and a machete, seen in the village, may have been used in cutting the tall growth. In the middle of the village is a typical "spoke fire," and on one of my visits a woman was cooking fish over the coals (pl. 9, c). Three or four thatched dwellings are here, and the women sit all day at their hand sewing machines, making garments for use or sale and usually listening to one of the small phonographs that are in many Seminole houses. A tame otter was flopping around the enclosure and on one occasion the construction of the thatched roof on a dwelling was seen.

TEMPORARY CAMP

On a trip from Miami to Everglades, we overtook a party of Seminole traveling in canoes on the canal that borders the Trail. They were about 10 miles east of Everglades and were Indians whom I had been desirous of seeing. The man, his wife, and two children were in the first canoe, and the second canoe, which was being towed, was loaded with utensils and camp equipment, neatly packed and covered with canvas. At the stern of this canoe were several small hides on stretchers, the hides not being fully dried before the party broke camp (pl. 14, b). The man kindly drew his canoe near shore while a picture was taken, and during this pause a large turtle that was being carried in the canoe almost made its escape.

The writer and her sister were traveling toward Everglades, and the Indians, as stated, were going in the same direction. On our return in the early afternoon the Indians were found camping on the opposite side of the canal. They had cooked and eaten the turtle, and the shell of the turtle, with the eggs, was seen in the fire according to the Seminole custom. Greetings were again exchanged, and in a short time they were probably on their way into the depths of the Everglades. A camp in the Everglades is shown in plate 14, a. Thatched roofs were seen in a temporary camp (pl. 10, b).

A contrast to the native villages is seen in the little group of dwellings at the Government station, 3 miles from Dania and 25 miles north of Miami. The Seminole were brought here from their village near Fort Lauderdale, which had become unsuitable for their use because of the encroachment of roads and commercial buildings. James L. Glenn,[6] officer in charge of the station in 1931–32, lived in a comfortable building erected to contain his living quarters, office, and the

---

[6] Mr. Glenn extended many courtesies to the writer which were helpful in her work.

schoolroom.   Six or eight small, one-room houses were erected for
the Seminole, whose children attend the school.   These houses are near
together, in a row, and at the farther end of the row is a thatched
structure like the native dwellings which is used for the storage of
various articles.   There is no shade near these houses, but the dense
growth of the region is back of them.

A typical Seminole village as seen from a dirigible is shown in plate
12, *b*, photographed by Claude C. Matlack.

EXHIBITION VILLAGES

The exhibition villages at Musa Isle and Coppinger's Tropical
Gardens are managed by white men, the Seminole living in native
dwellings.   The former village is the larger (cf. pl. 12, *a*), and a considerable portion of the material on the Seminole was gathered there,
in 1931 and 1932, through the courtesy of Mr. and Mrs. B. L. Lasher,
its owners and managers.   Contacts with the Indians were freely
given, together with the services of Cory Osceola, the interpreter.
Suitable places for recording songs were also provided (pl. 11, *c*).   A
Seminole wedding was witnessed at Coppinger's Tropical Gardens,
and a limited amount of information was obtained on other visits.

DWELLINGS

When the Seminole are in a temporary camp their shelter consists
of a slanting, thatched roof, one end resting on the ground and the
other supported by stout poles.   Their permanent habitation, in a
village or permanent camp, is a structure with a gabled roof and projections at each end, thatched with leaves of the Washingtonia palm
(pl. 11, *a*).   As the land in the Everglades is frequently flooded, the
Seminole raises the floor of his house about 2½ feet above the ground.
On this floor, or platform, the family sit or recline.   In the exhibition
villages the floors of the houses are of boards, but in a village in the
Cypress Swamp the floors of the houses are of logs, with surfaces
partly smoothed.   The houses at Musa Isle (pl. 12, *a*) were about 12
by 15 feet in size and a portion of the floor was cut away on the shorter
side, making it possible for the occupants to sit on the edge of the floor
and still be under the thatch.   The lower edge of the thatch was about
4½ feet above the ground.   The Seminole uses no mattresses or pillows,
and prefers "comfortables" to blankets.   These are rolled and placed
across the rafters during the day.   Sheeting or canvas curtains are
dropped around the sides of the house during rainy weather or at
night, if desired, and these also are stored on the rafters.   One of the
difficulties in changing from native customs will be the use of chairs,
as the women sit all day on the floor, working at their hand sewing

machines. Infants are often seen asleep in hammocks suspended from the rafters of a house, a strip of cloth attached to the hammock enabling the mother to swing it as she sits at her work.

An opportunity to watch the construction of a house was afforded on two different visits to Chestnut Billie's camp. Photographs were taken on both occasions. The frame of a house ready for the thatch was seen. In another section of the village a house was being thatched, and a man was arranging part of the palmetto leaves that form the thatch. The leaves extended below the edge of the roof, making an attractive shade at the side of the structure. They were nailed to the framework. A pair of logs, one on each side of the roof, is used to hold down the thatch. A man was seen adjusting one of these logs.

The houses of the Seminole are used only as living quarters, the cooking being done outside, or in a separate structure, and the food stored elsewhere. This, and the absence of any sort of furniture, make it possible for the people to live and work in a small space. The Semi-nole have not adopted the white man's satchel, suitcase, or trunk. Personal belongings are wrapped in cloth, and the only containers are cardboard cartons. The women are orderly, and able to pack their possessions to the best possible advantage. At Motlo's camp a woman was seen repacking clothing. Eighteen or twenty articles were folded square, one upon another, a man's trousers being folded smoothly and placed with the other articles. The stack of clothing was tied in a cloth. The wife of Cory Osceola wished to show a valued article and took a small box from the cloth bag containing her possessions. This she unlocked with a little key, carried on her person. The box and its contents were clean and neat.

CLOTHING AND ORNAMENTS

When a child is born a string of beads is placed around its neck. When a boy is "a certain number of moons old" the beads are re-placed by a small, three-cornered kerchief of soft fabric, tied in front. A little girl receives additional strings of beads from time to time, but, in childhood, does not wear enough beads to be a burden. A string of beads said to be suitable for a girl about 5 years old was obtained and found to be about three yards in length. Both boys and girls wear a one-piece dress with full skirt until they are about 3 years old, when a girl changes to a two-piece dress similar to that worn by the women (pl. 8, b). These little dresses are about ankle length and are of bright patchwork, like the garments of the adults (specimens were obtained). The one-piece dress is open in front and has a yoke and long sleeves, the waist and skirt being gathered into a belt. A little girl's dress is tied at the neck and often fastened with a safety pin at the waist, the placket in the skirt being about 2 inches long. The belt

is narrow, often ending in strips of cloth which are tied, fastening
the garment at the waist.

The one-piece style of dress is still worn by young boys and was formerly worn by the men. It is still worn by a few old men. The former
custom was that a man wore the ankle-length dress until he was about
50 years old, when he shortened the dress to knee length. Several
men wearing dresses below the knee were seen (pl. 9, a). Men with
shorter skirts are shown in plates 9, b, and 13, c. This costume was
adapted to the work of the men in former days. They tucked up their
skirts when wading in the water or working around their canoes. A
short, white cotton tunic, or shirt, is worn by some of the older men
(pl. 2, a). This is not a native costume and is said to have been adopted
from the white man's shirt, after trousers were worn. The old men
still wear cloth turbans which were formerly very large (pl. 2, a).
These differ in style but usually have one feather erect on the top. The
turbans are in a permanent form, being taken off and replaced without
disturbing the shape. When a man wears a felt hat he usually has a
colored band around it. The young men wear wide-brimmed, light
felt hats, of the type commonly called "cowboy hats." Several
costumes are seen in the family group in plate 8, a.

At the present time the young men wear black trousers and a full
blouse of patchwork like the dresses of the women. This blouse represents a transition in clothing, as it is like the old-fashioned dress
tucked into trousers. The sleeves are very full and gathered into a
band at the wrist. With the blouse is worn a soft neckerchief (pls. 1,
2, a, b; 3, a). A long scarf is also worn (pls. 3, b; 4, a). The blouse,
like the child's dress, has a square yoke bordered with strips of contrasting colors. In former times these color combinations were a
means of identifying members of a family, the custom resembling the
use of clan plaids in Scotland. The family colors were painted on
canoes.

Most of the adults and all the children are barefoot at the present
day, but seem to feel no discomfort in walking on the stones. Their
feet are not "spread," nor unsightly in appearance. The Seminole
women have very small feet; a trader stated that he thought no woman
in his village would wear a shoe larger than No. 3, while the average
size of a white woman's shoe is No. 5–7. An exception to those who
used no foot covering was an old man who wore buckskin moccasins,
with wrappings of the same material extending up to his knees.

A peculiar pair of moccasins, said to represent an old custom, was
obtained. The moccasin, made of buckskin, resembles an old-fashioned shoe in height and consists of two pieces, one for each side of
the foot, fastened together by a seam up the back and a gathered seam
up the front from toe to ankle. The moccasin is turned up at the

toe, has a small, loose piece of leather at the toe and heel, and is held in place by a thong around the ankle.

When a little girl lays aside the one-piece dress, she assumes the costume of a woman, which consists of a full skirt, an underwaist, and a cape of thin material gathered into a yoke of thicker cloth. In warm weather the underwaist is short, scarcely below the armpits and without sleeves, but in chilly weather the woman wears a waist with sleeves, extending below the waistband of her skirt. This garment preceded the cape, which has come into use during the past half century. Commodore Munroe remembers when the Seminole women did not wear the cape. The material preferred for a cape is thin voile of a plain color, but figured voile is used if the former cannot be obtained. Plain percale is used for two or three narrow bands on the edge of the cape and for the yoke, on which the decoration consists of a few narrow strips of colored cloth at the edge. Usually this decoration does not meet in the front, an undecorated space of a few inches being left (pls. 4, b; 6, a). The opening at the neck is large enough so that the cape is put on over the head. It is a sensible garment, affording protection and coolness while permitting free use of the arms. A woman conceals her hands under her cape when meeting strangers. (Cf. pl. 8, a, b.)

Many women wear handmade silver ornaments on their capes. These may be in the form of round disks, or buttons, sewed in place, or they may be pendants, which are often attached to the beads in the back. Earrings, finger rings, and bracelets of silver are worn in considerable quantity. The ears are pierced at an early age. At Dania an infant less than a month old was seen with pierced ears. The wearing of earrings is general, and one woman was seen "keeping the hole open" in another woman's ear by inserting a straw or small stick.

The decoration on Seminole garments formerly consisted of applique. This was of two sorts, one consisting of points of one color sewed on cloth of another color, and the other being a form of stencil. In this form of applique a diamond-shaped piece of cloth with a diamond-shaped opening in the center was placed over cloth of a different color and all the edges neatly sewed in place. Since the Seminole obtained hand sewing machines the applique has been replaced by the familiar patchwork banding. The making of this constitutes the chief industry of the women, and, as stated on page 33, the banding is in long strips, which are kept on hand, ready for use. These are commonly called "bands."

A woman wears two or three skirts, which are alike. Each is so long that it rests on the ground about 1½ inches, all around, and measures about 5 yards at the hem. The skirt is made of wide and narrow strips of percale in contrasting colors, plain cloth being preferred to figured material. Very narrow strips of different colors are frequently stitched on these plain strips. Two rows of "banding" are usually inserted in a skirt, and sometimes three are used, the widest being nearest the hem. At a point less than a foot below the waist, the width of the skirt is slightly reduced, being gathered into a somewhat narrower piece of cloth. This change in width is covered by a narrow ruffle of a strongly contrasting color. While the long seam up the back of a skirt may show some irregularities in the narrow bandings, most of the wide bandings are found to match with exactness. The upper edge of the skirt may be gathered into a band a few inches in width, or it may be finished with a narrow band, the ends of which are tied together in the back, holding the garment in place.

The strings of beads worn by the women extend from the ears to the shoulders, the upper strings being drawn tightly and firmly around the neck (pl. 4, *b*). A less careful arrangement of beads is seen in plate 6. Only one sort of bead is worn, this being smoothly round, opaque, and not very highly glazed. The favorite colors are dark blue and dull, pale green, but other colors are used and the combinations vary from day to day. Only some "foundation strings" are worn at night, and the arrangement of the strings of beads takes considerable time each morning. The writer has watched women select and put on the beads, trying different colors and taking them off until the effect is entirely satisfactory. The principal colors are at the upper edge and the lower border of the mass of beads. Since these are put on after the cape is adjusted and since the color combinations vary in the cape and dress, it is probable that the woman designs her beads to correspond with the dress she is wearing. A woman was seen putting on her beads, and kindly showed the writer how this was done. She was seated on the floor of her house and had a small mirror in front of her, propped against a pile of belongings. The beads worn by the women are bought in strings of uniform length, this being about 60 inches. The adjustment in length, when the beads are worn, is made by tying each double string together. Thus the strings of beads to be worn around the throat were measured the proper length, tied and adjusted, the stubby end of the original string being tucked inside the mass of beads. As the decoration reached her shoulders, longer strings were required, with less shortening of the original length. In the outer rows of the mass of beads that rested on her chest and shoulders, the original strings were used without being shortened. The skill in putting on the beads involves making each double string the proper length so the mass will be swooth, and also arranging the colors.

One woman kept her beads in a tin box at least a foot high and about a foot in diameter, the box being almost full of beads from which she was selecting those she wished to wear. The number of strings of beads worn by some women is so great that their necks are shriveled and their shoulders bent by the weight. Ornaments of pierced silver are sometimes attached to the beads in the back. As stated on page 16, one or two strings of beads are placed around a child's neck soon after it is born, and a girl wears the beads in increasing number as long as she lives.

Women do not remove their beads when they go in bathing. Neither do they remove their clothing, but deftly change their dresses when they leave the water.

HAIRDRESSING

The style of hairdressing among the women is neat and decorative. Their hair is long and is first combed straight up to the top of the head, so that the hair at the back of the head is flat and close. The mass of hair is then made into a smooth mat on top of the head by folding it back and forth, the line across the lower, back edge of this mat being horizontal (pl. 4, b). This mat of hair extends over the top of the forehead and is covered with a net made of black thread and decorated with small beads. There is a great variety in these nets, the beads being strung on the thread of which the net is woven and forming small, detached designs. As the hair of the women is black, the thread of the net does not show, and the beads, in their bright colors, are decorative and becoming. Some of the young girls wear a row of ordinary bone hairpins close together across the forehead, so that the loops of the hairpins form a decoration; others wear many of these pins around the mat of hair, the loop ends forming a decoration. Among the women there is also a custom of wearing "bangs" across the forehead, but this is not universal (pl. 6, b). In one camp a woman was seen dressing her hair in a "pompadour" by combing it over a pad made of a rag. At Chestnut Billie's Camp an old woman was seen doing her hair. She combed it to the top of her head, tied it, and made the ends into a loop which she pinned down with many bone hairpins.

CULTIVATION OF THE SOIL

The Seminole are "natural horticulturists," according to Mrs. Frank L. Stranahan, of Fort Lauderdale. Around their old village, with which she was familiar, they planted pineapples and mango and guava and orange trees. Many of these trees, in good condition, remain on the site of the village.

An old mill for crushing sugarcane was seen by the writer. It consisted of two vertical wheels, propelled by two long bars that were pushed by men.

In the Big Cypress group, each family has a little "farm" or garden in the Everglades where they cultivate corn and other vegetables, making it their home during part of the year (pl. 15, c). At other times they camp where the game is most abundant or where the occupation of the time may lead them.

It is said the Creeks raised the first tobacco in this region and that the Indians could secure tobacco seed at any grocery store. This was a poor quality of the white man's tobacco. The northern Seminole raided the Creek farms in the same way they raided the farms of white settlers.

PLANTING OF CORN

The Seminole plant their corn in February, the month designated in their calendar as the Big Moon month (p. 28). The women select particularly fine ears of corn during the harvest and store them for seed. Each family has a permanent camp near its little garden, and the corn is raised on a small patch of ground. When planting corn a man digs a hole with a sharp stick and a woman or little girl drops in the kernels. Sometimes boys help with this part of the work. Annie Tommie and her brother Willie Jumper are shown planting corn in this manner (pl. 16, b).

FISHING AND HUNTING

Fish are speared from the canoe. A man who had just thrown a spear for a fish was seen. Another man was seen with a three-tined spear for fish.

The game consists of otter, raccoon, bobcat, alligator, deer, and other animals. Ordinary steel traps are used in catching the bobcat and similar animals. As a lure for the deer it is customary to burn the grass on a little tract of firm land in the Everglades. Vegetation returns quickly, and the deer, attracted by the fresh, green sprouts, are killed while feeding. One method of catching an alligator is by slipping a noose around its jaws. By means of the rope it can be drawn toward the shore and lifted partially from the water. The animal is generally shot, but it may be killed with a knife or hatchet.

FOOD AND ITS PREPARATION

Fresh corn is boiled or roasted in the ashes. Many boil it without removing the husks. Dried corn is pounded in a mortar, which is made by burning and scraping out the center of a hickory log. The wood is so hard that no lining of the log or stump is necessary. The earliest implement for scraping out the center of the log was a large shell. The pestle is of hickory and the pounding of the corn is done by a woman, putting only a handful of the corn in the mortar at a time (pl. 16, *a*). The corn is pounded to various degrees of fineness and sifted through round basket sieves with meshes of several sizes. Palmetto leaves are used in making these sieves, the leaves being finely split for making the baskets with smaller meshes. The sides of such a basket are closely woven, also the bottom, except for a square opening which is filled by the lattice. Four of these baskets were obtained, the larger being 11 to 18 inches in diameter and the smaller being about 9 inches in diameter. The basket 11 inches across was 4½ inches in depth, with the usual square latticed opening in the bottom. (Like other specimens collected by the writer these are in the United States National Museum.) Larger baskets of the same shape are used as household containers.

The preparation of the "cabbage palm" for use as food was seen at Dania. This is the sabal palmetto, or cabbage tree. Missie Tiger cut a slit lengthwise of a stalk, and removed one layer after another. The center of the stalk was boiled. Water was obtained by digging a hole in the ground (pl. 5, *a*).

In a camp on the Tamiami Trail a woman was seen frying a "pancake" about an inch and a half thick in a skillet. She turned it by inverting the skillet on her hand and "flopping over" the pancake. It was not fried, as in northern tribes, but toasted on each side.

In Chestnut Billie's camp the women were baking biscuits in a Dutch oven of the usual type, with the fire on top of the cover. The biscuits looked wholesome when they were taken out. In a permanent camp there is a high table for the preparing of food.

Coontie, also called comptie, is a root that forms the most important factor in the food of the Seminole. A specimen of the root was obtained, and identified by Dr. J. Petersen of the Miami Botanical Gardens as *Zamia floridana*. Flour of two different qualities is made from this root, the process being photographed at Dania (pl. 18). Missie Tiger had gathered about a barrelful of the roots and was preparing them for her own use. They were gathered at the proper season, washed and scraped (pl. 18, *a*), and stored on a low platform under a thatch of palmetto, dry leaves being underneath and fresh leaves on the top. The platform was about 3 feet square and 2 feet in height. This storage is only until there is a convenient time for continuing the process. The roots are grated with a curved piece of tin with sharply edged holes, the tin being set on a board in such a manner that the grated roots fall between the tin and the board, sliding down to a piece of cloth spread on the ground to receive them. A woman grating the roots in a temporary camp on the Tamiami Trail is shown in plate 18, *b*. The resultant substance is placed in a barrel, water is added, and the whole is stirred with a long stick (pl. 18, *c*).

A small portion at a time is strained through a cloth, which is suspended from stakes at the corners. Water is occasionally added.
The powder is then dried. A few days later Missie Tiger was found
seated on the floor of her house beside a large cloth on which the flour
was slowly drying, and she was engaged in rubbing out the lumps so
that the flour would be smooth. This flour is generally of two qualities, the flour made from the outside of the root being a pale pinkish
brown and that from the center of the root being white. One informant said that a third quality was sometimes made and that it was quite
dark brown. Specimens of the first two qualities were obtained. The
taste was sweetish and not unpleasant.[7]

Two or three grades of flour were seen drying at Jim Gopher's
camp, the flour being spread on a cloth, laid on the floor. A thatched
cache of the roots was seen at this camp, and a cache of finished flour
in bags.

It is said that the war with the white man was greatly prolonged
because the Seminole understood the value of this native food.

A coarse variety of bananas known as "horse-bananas" grows wild
in the fields, and the Seminole also gather the ordinary bananas as
food.

The turtle is a favorite food of the Seminole. This is chiefly the
variety known as the "gopher turtle," which is abundant in the region. Both large and small turtles are eaten. Many turtle shells
were scattered near the camp at Dania. Missie Tiger said she had a
turtle in a box in her house, which she intended to cook soon. She
consented to be photographed holding this turtle. The turtle is usually boiled and the flesh eaten, or it is made into soup. In one camp a
woman was seen picking bits of crisped turtle meat out of the shell
as she sat beside a fire.

Cory Osceola stated that a large turtle is enough to serve 10 people,
and is boiled with potatoes, onions, and canned tomatoes. He also said
that a portion of a turtle is put in the fire. This was seen in a temporary camp on the Tamiami Trail. (See p. 14.)

The method of cooking depends on the circumstances under which
the people are living. The use of logs, arranged like the spokes of a
wheel, as described below, is limited to the permanent village or camp.
If the family are in a temporary camp, as when they are hunting,
the kettles are often hung from sticks thrust slantwise in the ground.

---

[7] A different method of preparation of the flour is suggested by the following: John C.
Gifford, in his book entitled "Billie Bowlegs," pictures a Seminole woman pounding "comptie" in a log, which is lying on the ground. Three apertures, or "mortars," are in the log
and a woman stands beside one of them, with a pestle which is her own height. This is
held by both hands and moved up and down. Two other pestles of the same length are
leaned against the log. This illustration appears to be a copy of an old photograph
(Gifford, 1925, illus. facing p. 74).

A family on a journey who had stopped to prepare a meal were seen cooking by a stream.

A "spoke fire" consists of 8 or 10 logs at least 6 feet in length arranged like the spokes of a wheel but not coming together in the center. There is a mound of ashes in the center, and a fire is kindled with small wood for cooking each meal. The logs are pushed forward when more heat is desired, or when the ends of the logs have burned off. Two or three families may cook with the fire. A woman sits on one of the logs when tending the kettles or preparing the food (pls. 9, c; 17, b). The logs for such a fire were seen in several villages in three sections of the Seminole country, including an unoccupied camp in the Everglades. Cooking under a thatched roof in a large village is shown in plate 11, b.

The cooking utensils of the Seminole are iron kettles obtained at the stores. Spoons both large and small are made of wood. The material chiefly used is the wood of the custard-apple tree, though a spoon made of cypress wood was obtained at Dania. A large spoon is used by the women in stirring kettles of food when cooking, and is the chief utensil used by the Seminole when eating. Seven of these spoons were obtained, some being very old and two being bought while in use, the Indian women taking them out of the corn porridge to sell them. The shape of the spoon used by the Seminole who live in the Big Cypress Swamp was slightly different from that of the spoon used by the Seminole at Dania who come from the Cow Creek band and from the old group near Fort Lauderdale. Both spoons had handles bent sharply near the end, but the spoons from near Dania were narrower and deeper. A "small spoon" was obtained and was about the size of our tablespoon. The large spoons were used by adults when eating and small children were seen eating with a spoon that would hold about half a teacupful.

When the food is cooked the kettles are taken from the fire, and the manner of eating depends on the circumstances. A family traveling on the canal, beside Tamiami Trail, were seen eating by their fire. In a camp visited in the cabbage palm region the people slept and ate on the ground. It is said that in the villages the men eat before the women. At Musa Isle there are three eating huts; two have "divided floors" and a third is an ordinary living hut. In the latter the men sat crosslegged around the kettles, on the platform. The older men were seen eating by themselves, and the young men often ate by themselves. Children of 6 to 10 years of age were seen eating together, under the supervision of two women. Very small children ate with a mixed group, including an old man, some women, and the fathers of the children. Babies were given bones to chew. The kettles were taken from the fire to the places where the food was to be eaten, and the people gathered around. There was nothing that resembled "setting the table." The food was taken from the kettles with a large wooden spoon and usually placed in granite cups. Plates were of granite, but were very rarely seen in the camps. Knives, forks, and metal spoons were not seen, and it was said that meat was eaten with the fingers.

The women seemed interested in their cooking, two or three women usually being busy in the cooking hut at Musa Isle in the middle of the day. It was observed that the noonday meal was on time. This was the only meal of the day, but food could be obtained at any other time if it was desired.

The food was varied. Indians were seen drinking corn porridge from a cup and removing the corn from the bottom of the cup with their fingers. Meat was cut into pieces and boiled in a considerable quantity of water, and meat and vegetables were seen in one kettle. Women were seen frying dough in a skillet, and eggs were also fried. Oranges were roasted in the coals. They were blackened on one side and resembled potatoes cooked in the same manner. They were eaten after peeling off the skin at one end. A child was seen drinking the milk from a coconut. A peculiar food was seen in a primitive village in the cabbage palm region. A woman was seated on the ground and beside her, at the top of a pole, were two or three objects resembling doughnuts, pierced by the pole. On being questioned, she said they were made of deer meat and melted fat and that she chewed them for food. One was obtained for the United States National Museum. No bread or other food purchased at a bakery was seen in the Seminole camps that were visited, but it is said that some camps in other localities are using such food when it can be obtained.

At the conclusion of a meal the kettles with the remaining food in them are left where the food was eaten, and are sometimes covered with a cloth. Anyone who wishes a lunch may help himself from the kettles, and this was often done. The utensils are usually taken to the cooking hut and put in a large pan of water until needed.

The cooking of fresh fish was seen, by chance, at Chestnut Billie's camp on the Tamiami Trail. An old man named Charlie Tiger came down the canal in a canoe with a large number of poles that Chestnut wanted to use in his camp (pl. 9, a). With the poles he brought four live fish. The women of the camp began at once to prepare them, the first step being to crisp them over the fire. It is always easy to secure fire for such a purpose as there are embers between the ends of the "spoke fire," and light wood is applied. Each fish was about 2 feet long. At first each fish was laid on a narrow board, and after it stiffened it was turned until both sides were crisped. The crisping was done with care, and when it was finished the fish were taken to a

26 BUREAU OF AMERICAN ETHNOLOGY [BULL. 161

place where such work was generally done. A woman sharpened her knife on a piece of wire netting, cut the head and tail from each fish, and skinned it with the knife. Then it was cleaned and cut into pieces about 3 inches long, and each section was split along the backbone. The woman then cleaned a kettle which contained similar pieces of fish, washed the fresh fish and put it in cold water, and then placed the kettle of fish on the fire (pl. 9, c). No vegetables were cooked with the fish. She then gathered up all the debris and threw it into the canal.

Fish was seen drying on the limb of a tree, in a temporary camp on the Tamiami Trail. Cory Osceola stated that meat as well as fish is dried in the sun, but neither is smoked over the fire.

Venison is pounded, mixed with melted fat, and stored in containers.

PREPARATION OF HIDES

The hides of small animals are stretched on frames or nailed on boards to dry. Several hides on frames were seen in the cabbage palm country (pl. 15, a). In Chestnut Billie's camp several hides were drying, a small hide being stretched on a board, leaning against a thatched platform, while a wildcat hide was nailed to a board, leaning against a tree. A family moving in two canoes carried two or three small hides nailed on boards, the hides not being fully dry. The Seminole manner of scraping a hide is shown in plate 7.

The hide of the deer is expertly tanned and is pale-cream color, with a soft texture. It does not appear that the tanning is done by women, as in northern tribes, but this was not a subject of special inquiry.

NAMES

NAMES CONNECTED WITH CLANS

The subject of "clan names" was not a matter of special inquiry, but Panther said his name is that of the clan to which his family belongs. He did not inherit this name, but received it. He cannot give this name to his son because it can be borne only by two living men, but after his death it will be the duty of his brother to give the name to some boy in the clan who is about 12 years of age.

NAMES CONNECTED WITH LOCALITIES

The names of the Seminole are identified with the part of Florida in which they live. Mrs. Frank L. Stranahan stated that the "east coast Seminole" were members of the Osceola, Jumper, Willie, and Tommie families. The Cow Creek group were the Tigers, Tigertail, and Parker families, the last being named for a cattleman. The Big Cypress people were the Billie and Cypress families. The Motlo family also belonged to this group.

MARRIAGE

Marriage with relatives is strictly forbidden. A marriage may be performed by any male relative of the bride or by one of the "old men of the tribe." Men frequently marry women older than themselves. The marriage of Cowboy Billie and Annie John took place recently. They were married by the father of the bride. On February 17 a Seminole wedding was seen at Coppinger's Tropical Village, and the following day a similar event was seen at Musa Isle and photographs were taken. On the former occasion the Catfish Dance was witnessed (cf. p. 120). Several old men came from the Everglades to attend the second wedding.

HOMELIFE

The homelife of the Seminole, as seen in the camps, seemed particularly pleasant. It is said that the Seminole are severe in the discipline of their children, and that it is usually necessary to use this discipline only two or three times, after which the child is tractable. I was told that the scarification of the arms was used as a punishment for children, and at Musa Isle one child was seen with scars from such scratches (see p. 29).

In a certain camp a little boy about 5 years of age was devoted in his care of a younger sister. If she fell down he helped her up and adjusted her little cape. A certain blind woman was always led by a little boy and girl who guided her with care. The boys and girls usually played by themselves in the various camps, and were quiet in their play.

The women are very affectionate in their manner toward small children. In one camp a little child was seen seated on an overturned pail while the mother cut its hair. Then it was given something to eat, and handed a toy.

Neatness in the care of personal belongings was noted in the camps and evidently taught to children. A little boy wanted a toy pistol to play with and was seen taking a cigar box from a rafter in his house. It contained his small belongings; he looked them over, took out the toy pistol, and repacked the others neatly, and then closed the box and replaced it on the rafter. Then he went away, playing with the little pistol.

WASHING OF CLOTHING

In old times clothes were washed by spreading them on a sloping rock beside a stream and pounding them with a piece of wood. At present the articles are spread on a sloping platform and thoroughly rubbed with soap, then rinsed in the stream and lifted out with a stick.

Washing in this manner was seen in Chestnut Billie's camp (pl. 15, *b*) on the Tamiami Trail and a washing platform was seen in the canoe-maker's camp. The clothing is spread on a fence or on the bushes to dry, forming a bright background to the camp scene.

CALENDAR

According to the custom of the Seminole the tribal year begins with the Corn Dance, but they also designate the months of the white man's calendar.

The months of the calendar begin with the winter solstice. The Seminole "watch a certain palm tree for the position of the sun and moon and make the months from the time when they turn in the other direction."

The names of the months in the white man's calendar are as follows:

Fubli (wind)_____	haci (little moon)_____	January.
Fubli (wind)_____	hastcobe (big moon)_____	February.
Biha cotci_____	Not translated_____	March.
Biha cobi_____	____do_____	April.
Buksa ci_____	____do_____	May.
Hayo tci_____	All small fruits ripe_____	June.
Haitco bi_____	All large fruits ripe_____	July.
Ota ci_____	Hot, no wind_____	August.
Ota cobi_____	Trees have berries on them_____	September.
Yo hobiha ci_____	No wind_____	October.
Klafta cobi_____	Big cold_____	November.
Hailing ci_____	Birds and fish frozen_____	December.

KNOWLEDGE RECEIVED IN DREAMS

A period of fasting is not required of a young boy, and he does not depend upon a dream in deciding to be a medicine man. However, he receives knowledge in dreams. Cory Osceola was very positive in this matter, saying "if a boy can't do it himself he is no *good*." He said that a boy does not tell his intention to be a medicine man unless he is asked, but "if he wants to find out something he goes to the old men and asks them about it." In this way he adds to knowledge that he has received in dreams. It was said, "everyone has useful dreams but some people have better dreams than others."

A Seminole may have help from the otter, panther, raccoon, bobcat, or other animal, and he may ask this "spirit helper" about things that trouble him, but no part of the animal is worn as a fetish. "The man just asks his helper if he wants to know something." A man does not bear a name indicating the identity of his "spirit helper." (Cf. p. 26 concerning clan names.)

Billie Stewart stated that the Seminole receive songs and a knowledge of medicines in dreams.

USE OF "PROTECTIVE MEDICINE"

In common with many other tribes, the Seminole believe in the power of an herb which is carried on the person or smoked in a pipe but not taken internally. Its power is not limited to medicine men. Panther, who is familiar with the "medicine practices" of the tribe, though not a "full medicine man," said that, in the old days, "A chief might send his boys in a canoe and they would be safe if they had this plant. They would smoke a little and carry it in a cloth. In war a man would not be hit if he had this herb." He said the herb is called "stingy man's tobacco." John Tiger gave the same information and a piece of the dried herb. "Stingy man's tobacco" was also smoked and carried by hunters to attract game. The protective use of bay leaves is described on pages 34–35.

AUTHORITY OF OLD MEN

The authority of the old men is severe and unquestioned (1932). For example, a certain young girl offended tribal standards by donning a bathing suit and going into the water at Musa Isle, in company with young girls of the white race. The older people heard of it and she "disappeared into the Everglades," remaining more than 6 months. The nature of her discipline was not told, but she emerged a demure Seminole maiden, in the voluminous dress of her tribe.

It is said that every 5 years the old men hold an "instruction for boys" and that this took place, in the Everglades, in 1931.

SCARIFICATION

The scarifying of the flesh on arms and legs is an old custom of the Seminole. This was said to be a punishment for children, but the custon included adults. It was one of the forms of punishment at the Corn Dance. J. B. Glenn, United States Indian Agent at Dania, said that he recently visited the northern part of the reservation, taking with him one of the most intelligent of the Seminole. When they were leaving, an old woman insisted that this man "scratch" the arms and legs of those present. He used a needle and exerted such pressure that the needle broke and had to be replaced. Even small children were subjected to this treatment. The flesh was thoroughly washed before being scarified and the blood flowed freely, but no medicine was applied. The only explanation was that the treatment would "make them brave."

Rows of round scars were seen on the arms of young women about 20 to 30 years of age. These scars were on both arms, and were distinct and of various sizes. Missie Tiger had about eight on each arm, arranged in a line and evenly spaced. The largest was near her wrist and about one-fourth of an inch in diameter. The others decreased regularly in size, the smallest being about half that diameter. She was not questioned concerning their significance.

PUNISHMENT

Punishment for crime is inflicted by a relative of the offender. One informant stated that for 5 days after a murder, the offender can be killed at sight by his relatives. After that time his punishment is deferred until the next Corn Dance. Another stated that as soon as possible after a crime the family of the offender assemble and decide the punishment to be inflicted. This punishment is usually in the form of whipping, administered by a relative—probably a distant relative. The man is tied to a post and whipped, the family council deciding the amount. This is said to be "reasonable" and the punishment is inflicted far in the Everglades, but the news spreads and the man is regarded in the same light as a white man who has been in prison. This informant said the only offenses punished at the Corn Dance are those that have occurred a short time before that event.

INDUSTRIES

CANOES AND THEIR MAKING

The canoes used by the Seminole are dugouts made of cypress logs. According to B. L. Lasher, it is the custom to burn around a cypress tree, letting the fire eat into the wood to the core. This makes a point at the foot of the tree, after which it can be felled easily. This point is used as the tip of the canoe. After the tree is on the ground, it is burned in two, forming the length of the canoe, the other end not being in a point. The inside of the log is hollowed out by fire, and the charred wood is scraped out. It is said that a large shell was once used for this purpose, but in recent times the Indians use a tool which may be described as a combination of an adz and a hammer. The blade is longer and wider than the claw of a hammer, is square across the end which curves toward the handle of the implement, while opposite is the ordinary head of a hammer. This is adapted for use on both the inside and outside of the canoe. (Pl. 8, c.)

No finishing is necessary on the outside of a canoe as cypress can stay in the water for an indefinite time without becoming waterlogged. If a canoe is made of cypress that has been attacked by worms (called "pecked cypress"), or if the log has a "split" in it, the wood is mended with pitch. A canoe that has stayed in the water a long time and becomes slimy on the surface makes less sound in the water than a clean canoe and is preferred for use in hunting.

A canoe is decorated with the "family colors," which are used also on dresses and on the yokes of men's blouses. These colors are applied to the inside of the canoe in broken stripes or angular patterns of contrasting colors.

A pole is used in propelling a canoe in the glades (pls. 9, *b*; 13, *c*) and sometimes a sail is used (pl. 14, *c*). Household goods are moved in canoes (pl. 14, *b*). Colors identifying families were formerly painted on canoes (cf. p. 17).

The canoes of the Seminole are of three general types: the canoe used long ago in deep water, the canoe used in the shallow water of the Everglades, and a wide canoe used in the glades for the transportation of families with their household goods. Models of these and of modified forms of these canoes were made by the Seminole. The oldest type of canoe was that used when the Seminole traveled in salt water, along the shore and between the shore and the nearby islands. This model was made by Billie Motlo and supplied with a sail and oars by Panther. This model was shown to Ralph Middleton Munroe,[8] an authority on marine architecture of this class, who stated that "the canoe embodies the best points of a boat for navigating rough water. It contains lines which can be interpreted only in formal terms of marine architecture. The flatbottom is adapted to landing on the beach, the oarlock is a very ancient device known as a becket, and the sail is the American type which came from old English patterns." The canoe, mast, and oars of the model are made of the wood of the custard-apple tree (*Annona glabra*). The twine holding the rigging in place is made from the green, inner bark of the same tree. The ropes used on such a canoe in the old days were made from the rubber tree (*Ficus aurea*), a specimen of such cord being made by Billie Motlo and included in the writer's Seminole collection.

John Tiger, an old man of the tribe, said that he remembered the use of these canoes and that travel on the Gulf was attended with some danger. He said "when the boys took a canoe out alone I gave them some of my medicine to carry, so they would be safe." He opened his medicine bag, showed a quantity of an herb resembling tobacco, and gave a few leaves to the writer.[9] The same herb was used as a charm for success in hunting.

Four other canoe models were made for the writer, one being painted in diamonds, according to the Seminole custom. It is thought the

---

[8] Ralph Middleton Munroe went to Key West in 1877 and has made his home in Coconut Grove since 1885. In the early days he contributed to the development of water communication along the Florida coast by designing and building boats of moderate displacement and limited draft. He was founder of the Biscayne Bay Yacht Club and commodore of the club for 23 years, still being known by that title. In collaboration with Vincent Gilpin, he is the author of "The Commodore's Story" (Munroe and Gilpin, 1930). Commodore Munroe died on August 26, 1933.

[9] The leaves obtained from John Tiger were identified by Dr. Gilbert, of the University of Miami, Miami, Fla., as *Nicotiana rustica* L. Information concerning the plant is as follows: "*N. rústica* (wild tobacco), still cultivated by the Indians of the eastern States, is of uncertain origin" (Encyc. Brit., 1937 b, vol. 16, p. 430). Nicotiana rústica L. "Said to be the first species of tobacco introduced into Europe. Its use was made known by John Nicot for whom the genus was named" (Bailey, 1935, vol. 2, p. 2143).

painted canoe was made by John Tiger, while he was still able to use tools (his death occurred during the present work, p. xxvii). Two of the others were made by Billie Motlo and one by a brother of Cory Osceola. The tool used in making these models, and in similar wood working is a curved knife, made from the blade of a steel table knife, shortened and turned horizontally, the handle being wrapped in rags. This is somewhat similar to the curved knife used by the Chippewa, but the blade is turned much farther, being turned to form almost a circle. Like the Chippewa knife, it is drawn toward the worker.

These four canoes are different in their lines. The painted canoe is much wider and higher at the prow than the others and such a canoe would be suitable for moving household goods; one of the smaller models is of this type but the lines are less exaggerated. The other two represent the long, slender canoe used in the Everglades, one model being larger than the other. With the smaller model is a pole, or "canoe pusher" of appropriate length.

The camp of John Osceola, a canoemaker, was visited. This camp is in the cypress woods, some distance back from the Tamiami Trail, and a narrow waterway has been constructed from his camp to the canal, for the passage of his canoes. In the camp a partly finished canoe was seen, resting on logs. The chips were beneath it, and between the canoe and the water was a sloping platform, used for launching the canoes and also for the washing of clothes by the women. John Osceola is also known as Captain Tony.

In Chestnut Billie's camp, on the Tamiami Trail, a canoe was seen and measured. This canoe was 25 feet and 5 inches in length. At a point 3 feet and 1 inch from the stern it was 1 foot and 10 inches in width. At a point 1 foot and 5 inches from the bow it was 1 foot and 5 inches in width. Near the end of the bow it was 1 foot 6½ inches in height.

A canoe with a sail was seen on the canal beside Tamiami Trail (pl. 14, c). The mast was across the middle of the sail, and a rope extended from each corner of the sail. A pole held the sides of the sail taut, and a boy held the ropes, managing them so as to catch the wind and steer the canoe. As he paddled the canoe out from shore, he put the ropes under a short slit in the side of the canoe. When he reached the middle of the canal he took the ropes and resumed the steering of the canoe.

The canoe is handled in a variety of ways, according to convenience. Thus a man was seen poling a canoe stern forward. A girl was seen sitting in the stern of a loaded canoe, paddling it.

SILVERWORK

The women wear earrings, finger rings, and bracelets of silver, as well as buttons and disks fastened to their capes or beads. The native work is pierced or pounded, and designs are never etched on the surface. The ornaments are always flat, the silver never being bent or twisted. The Maltese cross is a design frequently seen in ornaments. A pair of pendant silver earrings, worn by a Seminole woman, showed a design of a boat with a sail inside a circular border.

CARVING OF WOODEN DOLLS

The Seminole are experts in wood carving, and two types of wooden dolls with carved heads were obtained. Dolls carved of wood, about 2 inches long, were formerly made as toys. Another is a greatly elongated figure made by a woman who seldom comes out of the Everglades. Both dolls are dressed in the costume of Seminole women.

MAKING OF PATCHWORK BANDING

The cotton cloth used in making patchwork banding is fine, firm in texture, and preferably plain in color. Black is used more than white in the patchwork, white being never used as a foundation color while black is often employed in that manner. Pale green and mauve are preferred to blue or pink, but the favorite colors are red and yellow, with black as a contrast. The cloth is torn in strips and cut into blocks of the desired size and shape. For this purpose the women use very fine, sharp scissors with long, slender blades. The blocks are placed in little piles, each size by itself, ready for use. Thus a woman was seen with several piles of small squares and triangles near her left hand, on the edge of her sewing machine, where she could put them under the needle in the desired order, without basting. The women work at this task for many hours at a time, often with a phonograph playing as they work. The banding is made in long strips which are folded away, ready to be inserted in skirts and blouses, or in dresses for little children or old men. The width varies as well as the pattern. Ordinary designs consist of little squares of light and dark material, like a checkerboard, or small triangles of contrasting colors. Upright stripes alternating with horizontal stripes produce a pleasing pattern. Long, narrow triangles are used effectively, and the patterns in wide banding are surprisingly elaborate and original. The material and the finished banding are kept scrupulously clean, and the women are always neatly dressed when at work, with everything orderly around them.

WOVEN BEADWORK

The technic of weaving beads on a warp of thread is similar to that of the northern tribes, but the loom is like a shallow bottomless box instead of a thin frame. Two of these looms were seen in the Seminole camps. The boards comprising the boxlike loom are about 2½ inches wide, and the looms are about 8 by 20 inches in size. The weaving was a band about 1½ inches wide, and a favorite pattern embodied a United States flag. No native pattern of applied design was seen in the handicraft of the Seminole. These woven bead bands, in the form of belts or small articles, are sold to tourists. None were seen in use by the Seminole.

DEATH AND BURIAL

There is no subject on which it is more difficult to obtain information than the customs pertaining to the disposal of a body after death. It is commonly known that the body is taken into the Everglades and left there, but the details are hidden. Certain white men, however, have been present on such occasions, and their statements are given, together with statements by two white women who have long been in contact with the Seminole. From these narratives it is possible to form a reasonably clear idea of the procedure. There seems to be a wide variance in the custom, so that a complete account can scarcely be obtained.

Among the writer's oldest informants was John Tiger, one of the most prominent old men of the tribe. He remembered when the Seminole traveled in canoes on Biscayne Bay, and he opened his medicine bag, giving the writer a piece of the herb that in old times was carried for safety on the water (see p. 31). His medicine bag was a square of dingy cloth containing about a double handful of leaves. Panther said these were leaves of "stingy man's tobacco." (Cf. p. 29.) Knowing the Indian custom, the writer gave him a moderate sum of money and promised a gift. Panther, who interpreted the conversation, said that a white handkerchief would be an acceptable gift, and it was brought the following day.

John Tiger was in frail health at that time and, his condition becoming worse, he was taken to a hospital in Miami. Before he left Musa Isle his hair was cut close to his head. The writer called upon him in the hospital. His death occurred January 1, 1932.

The following information was supplied by B. L. Lasher who accompanied the body to the Everglades. With him was Captain Pope, these being the only white persons in the party. Early on the morning after the death of John Tiger, his body, in a casket, was taken some distance on the Tamiami Trail, put in a canoe, and taken into the Everglades. The casket was carried by means of a long pole, fastened lengthwise above it. Panther had charge of the procedure and chewed bay leaves and spat on the three men who carried the casket "to give them strength and to ward off evil spirits." Bay leaves were carried by all who went into the Everglades. When the party reached its destination, Panther again chewed bay leaves

and spat on the casket. John Tiger's belongings were laid on
top of the casket, which was then covered with leaves and branches
held in place by logs. It was said the body would remain there not
longer than 30 days and would then be carried to its final resting
place, farther in the Everglades.

On the next day the writer visited the Musa Isle village. An old,
dark-blue cloth was hung in John Tiger's house, enclosing in a square
the place where he used to sit. Possibly his widow was thus screened
from view. Three women and two men were weeping profusely, the
women covering their faces with their capes and the men showing
intense grief. The women's hair was hanging loose. The next day
it was said that Mrs. Tiger had gone into the Everglades and would
not return for 6 weeks. The immediate family also went away, and
their house passed to other occupants.

During the weeks that followed, all the women related to John
Tiger wore their hair loose, and some were seen with only a few
strings of beads. The loosened hair was seen also at Dania and another
Seminole village, the mourning being general among his relatives.

The following narrative was supplied by L. M. Rawlinson, of
Okeechobee, Fla. Mr. Rawlinson's father was one of the earliest
settlers of Okeechobee, and he has been acquainted with the Seminole
all his life. Willie John, a Seminole, died in a temporary camp at
Parker's Branch, near Blueville, Fla., in December 1931, and Mr.
Rawlinson was asked to convey the body in his truck to its final
resting place. Another white man went with him. On going to the
place they found the body a short distance from the camp. It was
encased in thick wrappings which might have been blankets, and outside these was heavy canvas. Around this long packet were strips
of heavy denim about 14 inches apart, each strip being tied. It was impossible to tell at which end of the packet was the head of the body.
On top of this packet was a pole that projected at least a foot at each
end. The pole was tied to the packet and had been used by the
Seminole in carrying it from the camp to the place where it was seen.

The coffin was a box made of heavy cypress boards. This was taken
from the truck and placed beside the body. The pole was lifted and
laid at one side, but care was taken to keep it parallel with the body.
After the body had been placed in the coffin, a branch of bay tree was
brought. Leaves were taken from this branch and strewn on the
entire length of the body. A quantity of kettles and utensils and a
bundle apparently containing clothing were put in the box, an equal
portion being put at each end. The top of the coffin was then nailed
in place, the coffin was placed on the truck, and the pole was laid on
top of it in exactly the former position.

In starting for the place of disposal it was said that a place in a
swamp would be selected, so that the body would not be molested by

the fires that burn the palmetto on the dry land. After traveling north for some distance they came to a cabbage palm hammock with a creek beside it. The party turned and went about 20 feet eastward, indicating the desired place.

A cabbage palm was felled, and two pieces about 3 feet long were cut and placed on the ground as supports for the ends of the coffin. The branch of bay leaves from which leaves had been removed was never laid on the ground, a man handing it to another when he took the ax to chop the tree. Thus it was handed back and forth, as the men took turns in the task of chopping. When the coffin was laid on the logs, the pole remained on top of it and the whole was covered with palmetto leaves.

Two women arrived, one being the sister of the dead man. A small tree of "light wood" was then cut, and small pieces, like splinters, were cut and given to these women, who made a fire of them, not far from the body.

When the box had been partly covered with palmetto leaves Mr. Rawlinson and the other white man withdrew, leaving the Indians alone with their dead.

Other informants said that personal belongings are left with the body, which is covered with interspaced poles like the roof of a house, and that a small fire of twigs is built near the head. It was also said that the widow remains at the place 4 days and nights, wailing, with disheveled hair, and that, if she has children, they stay with her. Further information was to the effect that the Seminole never return to the place where a body has been left, and also that when a widow resumes her beads and arranges her hair it is understood that she is ready to remarry.

Mrs. Frank L. Stranahan, of Fort Lauderdale, whose husband was a trader among the Seminole, recalled an incident which came under her personal observation. A Seminole girl fell dead in the door of her husband's store one evening. She said it was the Seminole custom not to move a body until it is taken for final disposition, so the body of the girl remained where it fell until the next morning, when a company of men started away with it. She said that the immediate family never accompanied the body but followed 3 days later. (It will be recalled that the relatives did not accompany the body of the dead in the previous narratives.) Wild myrtle was always burned in front of a burial company, bay was often used, and the burial place was always approached from the west, no matter in what direction the party had come from the camp.

On the day after this death, the women, girls, and boys sat on a log facing the East and did not move during the entire day. All were stripped to the waist, and the women had their hair loosened. A medicine man sat near the house. He had a pail of water and blew into the water through a reed, then he sang and sprinkled the water on the mourners, repeating this during the entire day (cf. p. 171 in which medicine is thus treated for the dying).

The custom of placing food with a body or on a grave was mentioned by two informants in the northern region. The Rev. E. M. C. Dunklin of Okeechobee said that he saw an instance in which bacon as well as kettles was put with the body of the dead. Mrs. Eliza Fielden, of Brighton (see p. 11), about 17 miles west of Okeechobee, said she knew of an instance in which food was taken to a grave daily for 3 days. The distance was several miles and the food was taken each day by a different person, in the cool of the morning. She also recalled an instance in which a coffin was left open for 3 days, and the disposal of the body made on the third day. In another case a man died away from home and his friends brought all his belongings in a sheet, saying "Put that in the box." They brought a gun and two shells, it being the invariable custom to put two shells in a coffin with a gun.

Mrs. Fielden has lived in close touch with the Seminole for 8 years and said the disposal of a body is always east of the place where death occurs.

The following incident may be mentioned at this time, as it came under Mrs. Fielden's personal knowledge. A man was recently very ill, and his condition became so serious that the Indian Agent decided to have him taken to a hospital. The man was in a dying condition but the Indians had drenched him with water and were walking around him as he lay in this state. He was dried, wrapped, and taken to a hospital, where he died in a short time.

An old Seminole burial ground, near Fort Lauderdale, was visited and photographed. Mrs. Frank L. Stranahan escorted the writer to this spot, saying that she and her husband visited it frequently, many years ago, and that he knew the locations of several graves. This burial ground was used by Indians in the village near Fort Lauderdale, before these Indians were removed to the Indian Agency near Dania, a few years previously. The site of this village was near a road which had become a traveled highway, and large buildings had been erected across the road from the old burial ground. Some of their fruit trees remain on the village site. In recent times the burial ground has been visited by many persons seeking relics of various sorts.

MISCELLANEOUS NOTES

The Seminole are not large in stature, but are of good physical appearance. The women have small hands and feet, carry themselves well, and have an indefinable air of daintiness in spite of the voluminous dresses. The motions of their hands are graceful. Their complexion is a clear brown. The type of face varies greatly, and it is said that some have slanting eyes. This peculiarity is seen in the portrait of a young woman (pl. 6, *b*). Sam Willie and son (pl. 3, *b*), Mrs. Tiger tail (pl. 6, *a*), and a family group (pl. 8, *a*) are typical members of the tribe. The manner of the Seminole is gentle, and they appear to be pleasant in their relations with one another. Their voices are generally low, and their language is musical in sound, with smooth vowels. They frequently laugh aloud among themselves, which is not a custom in other tribes. Some women were heard talking in thin, piping, high-pitched voices, but the occasion was not known.

Smoking was seen among the women, but not among the men. Young women were seen smoking cigarettes a few times.

White cloth was not seen in household use.

It is considered bad luck to kill any except poisonous snakes.

The use of a knife in making a small canoe was seen in one of the camps. A man held the knife like a pencil, with the thumb and first finger over the knife, braced by the second finger. Holding the knife in this position, he drew it toward him.

The Seminole have portable phonographs in many of their houses, and these are often of good quality. The records heard are usually monologs interspersed with songs, these being in southern (not Negro) dialect. Records of "cowboy songs" are popular. It is said the Seminole learn to speak English by listening to these records.

The hurricane of September 18, 1926, was predicted by the Seminole. Dr. Gifford said that the Indians of Okeechobee warned him 4 days before the event and he transferred all the people in his charge to a safe place, thus being entirely prepared for the catastrophe. In the neighborhood of Miami, it was told that Big Sam Willie said three times "Pretty soon water go over this trail" (referring to the Tamiami Trail). The Indians began moving to higher ground, and not an Indian was there when, about 30 days later, the water rose and covered the trail. Large numbers came to Musa Isle as a refuge. Such high water was exceedingly rare at that season. A Seminole called Bill said to Sam Willie, "How know?" The reply was "Moon tell me."

The Seminole living in the interior of the Everglades use vegetable dyes, according to Cory Osceola.

MUSICAL INSTRUMENTS

RATTLES

It appears that the rattle is the oldest musical instrument of the Seminole, as Billie Stewart said he had heard of a time when the

Seminole had no drum—only the coconut-shell rattle. Panther stated this rattle was used in the old wars. In the social dances the accompanying instrument is the coconut-shell rattle, similar to the gourd rattle used in many tribes. It consists of a coconut shell, pierced by a stick and containing the seeds of the *Canna flaccida* Roscoe. A pod of this plant was obtained and identified by Dr. John C. Gifford, whose assistance is acknowledged with appreciation. The women who take part in the Corn Dance and Stomp Dance wear rattles tied around each leg, below the knee (cf. pp. 45–46). Formerly a string of small turtle shells was used for these rattles, each shell containing small pellets of mud, made by hand and hardened by exposure to the sun. At the present time tin cans are similarly used, pierced with holes that are smaller than the mud pellets. Such rattles were worn by the women in a Catfish Dance witnessed by the writer.

DRUMS

A small hand drum is the accompanying instrument with the songs of the Corn Dance. This was said to be an ordinary drum of this type, with one head.

A "cypress knee drum" is the accompanying instrument with the songs of the Stomp Dance. (Cf. p. 107.) A "water-drum" is used with songs of the ball game. (Cf. p. 187.)

FLUTES

The use of a flute among the Seminole is traditional, but difficulty was experienced in finding anyone who remembered it definitely. Jim Gopher, a Cow Creek Seminole living near Dania, remembered hearing a flute but could not make one. Billie Stewart, however, was able to make a flute. A piece of suitable cane was obtained at the Botanical Gardens near Miami, through the courtesy of Dr. J. Petersen, owner and manager of the Gardens. The flute, now at the United States National Museum, contains peculiarities not previously noted in an Indian flute. The removal of the septums of the cane is like that in other flutes, but the detached piece that forms the "whistle head" is flush with the tube instead of being in the form of a block or band above the opening. It is tied in place with a buckskin thong, as in the flutes having a wooden block.

This flute has four fingerholes spaced in about the usual manner but its outstanding peculiarity lies in the boring of two holes transversely through the cane at right angles to the sound holes and equally distant from them, the transverse holes occurring between the locations of the fingerholes. It is further noted that the edges of the fingerholes are beveled. This is unusual and permits a tight sealing of the finger, stopping the hole completely. The fingerholes were burned with an iron and the beveling done with a knife. The bore is neat and is made the length of the cane except for the obstruction at the whistle head.

Concerning-the use of a flute by the Seminole, Bartram says the instrument is "made of a joint of reed or the tibia of the deer's leg; on this instrument they perform badly, and at best it is rather a hideous melancholy discord, than harmony. It is only young fellows who amuse themselves on this howling instrument" (Bartram, 1793, pp. 502–503). This observation by a man who heard the instrument played at an early day is exceedingly valuable. It would probably be impossible to find any Seminole at present who could play the cane flute.

A further historical reference to this type of instrument is of interest. Strachey states, concerning the East Coast Indians, "They have a kynd of cane on which they pipe as on a recorder, and are like the Greeke pipes which they call *bombyces*, being hardly to be sounded without great strayning of the breath" (Strachey, 1849, p. 79). The term "recorder" refers to the recorder flute that was held in a vertical position, like the clarinet of the white man.

CORN DANCE

The only tribal gatherings of the Seminole are the Corn Dance in June and the Hunting Dance held in September. Certain dances are given by the Cypress Swamp and Cow Creek groups on these occasions as well as a large number of social dances. The occasions for dancing, apart from the formal gatherings, were not described, but it was said that some dances could be given at any time while others were designated as "summer dances" and "winter dances."

The Corn Dance in the Cypress Swamp group was described and its songs recorded by Charlie Billie, who is the leader in that group, and Panther, who is prominent in the ceremony. Billie Stewart, leader in the Cow Creek group, described its customs, recording the songs. As the details of the ceremony were not a subject of investigation, no attempt was made to combine or compare these descriptions. In both groups the leaders were said to fast for a day before the ceremony, which opened with the Buffalo Dance. Many other phases are common to both groups. In 1931 the Corn Dance was held at three places, no two dances being held at the same time.

CYPRESS SWAMP GROUP

Charlie Billie described the Corn Dance in January 1931, and recorded the songs that he sings as leader of the ceremony. Cory Osceola acted as his interpreter and added to the information. Work on the subject was resumed in November of the same year and Panther recorded songs and described the ceremony.

The Corn Dance is held in June, as stated, "after the corn is ripe and when everyone can get together." In a recent year it was held June 22. Communication is slow in the Everglades and some families may be detained longer than others on their farms, or they may live at a greater distance, but no one eats any of the new corn until after the ceremony. Cory Osceola said "We always have the Corn Dance for our Thanksgiving." According to this informant, the dance is held in a place that is accessible only to the Seminole. In order to reach the place it is necessary to go up a shallow stream and walk in the water part of the way. It is said that W. Stanley Hanson, of Fort Myers, is the only white man who has witnessed the Corn Dance and sat in the councils of the Indians held at that time. The duration of the dance is usually 4 to 8 days. Several years ago a performance called a Corn Dance was given publicly in Miami, but was admitted to be a false presentation of the ceremony.

The leader of the singing and dancing is chosen, the position not being hereditary. Charlie Billie is the leader in this group at present (1931), as already stated. In his position as leader he wears no ceremonial garments or articles but is well dressed, probably having some new clothing made for the occasion. He recorded the four principal songs of the ceremony and a fifth that is used in the general dancing. Concerning the four songs he said, "When singing these at a Corn Dance I do not eat that day nor the night after," indicating that they belong to the period of fasting which precedes the ceremony. The songs are sung only on that day. When leading the songs of this dance, he and his "helper" pound on small hand drums which have one head. Charlie Billie sings the song once, then his helper sings it with him, and then everyone joins, dancing in a circle. These songs were not transcribed owing to an accident that befell the cylinder record.

In the Cypress Swamp group the Corn Dance is the time for the trial and punishment of offenses that have not been tried and punished by the families of the offenders (cf. p. 30). The punishments were said to consist of whipping and cutting gashes in arms and legs. W. Stanley Hanson, who has been present at the Corn Dance, said that he was asked "not to look" when these punishments were inflicted. The subject of punishment was not mentioned by the Cow Creek informants, but it is probable that the custom extends throughout the tribe.

For 3 or 4 days, while the people are gathering for the Corn Dance, those who wish to dance may do so for 2 or 3 hours in the evening. During the Corn Dance there is dancing most of the day and part of the evening, and on the night before the people disband they dance until morning. The dance lasts from 4 to 8 days, according to the time that the people can remain together.

On the morning before the Corn Dance, the medicine men begin a fast which continues until the next morning. Men and boys may share in this fast, but the boys usually eat some food that night. The number of medicine men must be 4 or multiples of 4, the usual number being either 4 or 8. In the early evening of this day a "sacred bundle" is opened and the contents exposed to view for about 10 minutes. Billie Motlo (pl. 2, *a*) owns one of these bundles and opens it at the Corn Dance. The medicine men are seated in a row, with the bundle in front of its owner. A fire, with a kettle of medicine, is in front of them, and beyond is another fire around which the people move in the Buffalo Dance, after the opening of the sacred bundle. Panther is not a "full medicine man," as stated on page xxv, but he has "worked 4 years" with the bundle, his place being second from the left, as the men sit facing the bundle. He has also worked the same length of time "around the kettle of medicine." His exact duties in either position were not a subject of inquiry. At the ceremony he wears a long shirt of cloth and a cloth coat, with buckskin moccasins and leggings. Twenty-five years ago the men wore large turbans, in which eagle feathers were stuck.

Panther said that the medicine man who owns the bundle "sings and talks about long life" when the bundle is opened, but does this so softly that no one hears him plainly. Everyone keeps still while he opens the bundle, talks, and sings. All the medicine men are close around him, and other men may see the contents of the bundle, but no women are allowed to come near. The sacred articles are spread on the white deerskin in which they are wrapped. These articles include four or five sorts of herbs and an ear of corn on the end of a stick. Neither the ear of corn nor the stick is decorated, and the same ear of corn is used year after year. While the bundle is open, the stick with the ear of corn is placed in the ground, pointing toward the east.

BUFFALO DANCE

After the bundle has been closed, the men and women dance the Buffalo Dance which continues about 10 minutes and has only four songs. Panther said this was the first dance that the Indians had and that it originated in the following manner: A great many young men had been sent out to hunt and get food for the people. They returned with buffalo, deer, bear, and tiger, and then the people "figured out" this dance. The head men of the Wing and Panther clans "worked together" and led the dance. For this reason the singer, as a member of the panther clan, leads the dance wearing a belt of panther hide with the tail hanging down behind. He has a drum, which is usually slung over one shoulder, and this is the only accompaniment of the songs. He sings the songs, and everyone joins in the vocalizations that precede and follow the songs. Carrying the drum, he leads a double line of singers, two men being followed by two women, and couples alternating in this manner. They move around the fire, in a contraclockwise direction. The songs are four in number, as stated, and are very old, the meaning of the words being unknown.

The Buffalo Dance was witnessed at a Seminole wedding, at Coppinger's Gardens, near Miami, on February 17, 1932, and three of its songs were heard on a similar occasion at Musa Isle, on the following day. In the songs at Musa Isle, Panther sang the first phrase of the song, then the people repeated it, and then Panther sang with them. He also sang one of the songs alone.

No. 1. Buffalo Dance Song (a)

(Catalog No. 2080)

Recorded by PANTHER

No. 2. Buffalo Dance Song (b)

(Catalog No. 2081)

Recorded by PANTHER

No. 3. Buffalo Dance Song (c)

Recorded by PANTHER

(Catalog No. 2082)

No. 4. Buffalo Dance Song (d)

Recorded by PANTHER

(Catalog No. 2083)

During the night the medicine men and others who wish to join them drink the medicine that has been brewed in the kettle. This is both an emetic and a purgative.

CORN DANCE

Two sets of Corn Dance songs were recorded by Panther. These were sung only in the evening and are the most important songs of the gathering. It seems probable they were sung after the Buffalo Dance songs on the night preceding the event, but the information is not clear on this point. Each set consists of four songs, and the dancers rest after singing the set. The words are obsolete and their meaning is unknown, as the songs are very old. The leader sings one phrase, then all join in the singing, as noted in the performance of the Buffalo Dance songs heard at Musa Isle (p. 43). There is no drum, but the sound of rattles worn by the women is heard, marking the time. These rattles are tied around each leg, below the knee. Formerly a string of small turtle shells was used for these rattles, each shell containing small pellets of mud, made by hand and hardened by exposure to the sun. At the present time tin cans are similarly used, pierced with holes that are smaller than the mud pellets. The cans

No. 5. Corn Dance Song (a)

(Catalog No. 2084)

Recorded by PANTHER

Fine

thus used are about 5 inches in height, and two cans, wrapped in a cloth are tied around each leg of the dancer. A pair of these rattles was obtained from a woman who had worn the rattles many times in the Corn Dance. She demonstrated her ability to wear them without any sound, as she would do when walking to join the dance circle, and she also showed their sound when she was dancing. This sound was more musical than a majority of rattles, and a considerable number of women, all wearing such rattles, would provide a pleasing accompaniment for the songs. This woman lived in the Seminole village near Dania.

The procedure of the Corn Dance is entirely different from that of the Buffalo Dance. The leader of the singing is also leader of the line of dancers in which men and women alternate. The dancers usually hold hands, thus forming a long line, and the motion is contraclockwise, around the fire.

No. 6. Corn Dance Song (b)

Recorded by PANTHER

(Catalog No. 2085)

Fine

No. 7. Corn Dance Song (c)

Recorded by PANTHER

(Catalog No. 2086)

No. 7. Corn Dance Song (c)—Continued

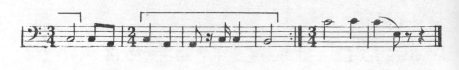

No. 8. Corn Dance Song (d)

(Catalog No. 2087)

Recorded by PANTHER

No. 8. Corn Dance Song (d)—Continued

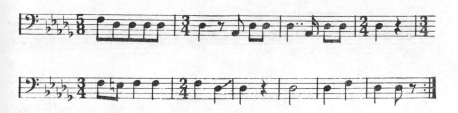

No. 9. Corn Dance Song (e)

Recorded by PANTHER

(Catalog No. 2088)

No. 9. Corn Dance Song (e)—Continued.

Fine

No. 10. Corn Dance Song (f)

(Catalog No. 2089)

Recorded by PANTHER

Fine

No. 11. Corn Dance Song (g)

(Catalog No. 2090)

Recorded by PANTHER

No. 11. Corn Dance Song (g)—Continued

No. 12. Corn Dance Song (h)

(Catalog No. 2091)

Recorded by PANTHER

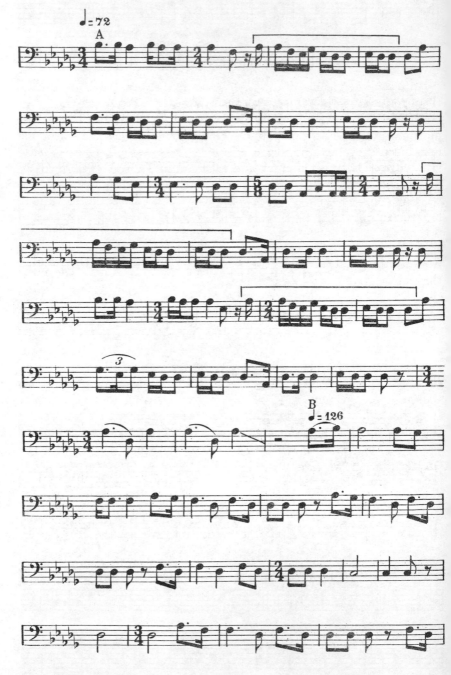

No. 12. Corn Dance Song (h)—Continued

COW CREEK GROUP

Billie Stewart, leader of the Corn Dance in the Cow Creek group, was the informant on the subject.

The fast that precedes the Corn Dance in this group is from one morning until the next morning. This is a discipline of the medicine men but others, including boys, may join. It was said, however, that "the boys usually get hungry and eat at night." All are allowed to drink a little water during their fast. Early the next morning all who wish may enter the sweat lodge where "medicine" is sprinkled on four heated stones with a wisp of brush. It is probable that medicine is taken internally, according to the custom in other tribes, as it was said that "some people feel well all summer after taking the sweat bath and medicine at the Corn Dance." After leaving the sweat lodge they swim in cold water and eat breakfast.

BUFFALO DANCE

The Buffalo Dance begins as soon as the medicine men are ready— sometimes about 4 o'clock in the morning—and continues until noon. Long ago the men wore the horns and hide of the buffalo in this dance, in which men and women join. The songs are accompanied by the shaking of a coconut shell rattle, the rhythm being that of a triplet of eighth notes with strokes on the first and second and a rest on the third divisions of the triplet. This was heard in the rendition but not recorded, therefore the tempo and rhythm are not indicated in the transcription. Four songs of the Buffalo Dance were recorded, but only two were transcribed.

No. 13. Buffalo Dance Song (e)

(Catalog No. 2384)

Recorded by BILLIE STEWART

No. 14. Buffalo Dance Song (f)

(Catalog No. 2317)

Recorded by BILLIE STEWART

MEDICINE MEN'S DANCE

On the first day of the Corn Dance a certain dance is performed four times. This is known as the Medicine Men's Dance and may be repeated at any time during the summer, but it is always preceded by a fast of 1 day and an entrance into the sweat lodge. The same fasting and dance precede the Hunting Dance in the fall, but at that time there is no entrance into the sweat lodge. The four songs of this dance were recorded.

No. 15. Song of Medicine Men's Dance (a)

(Catalog No. 2172)

Recorded by BILLIE STEWART

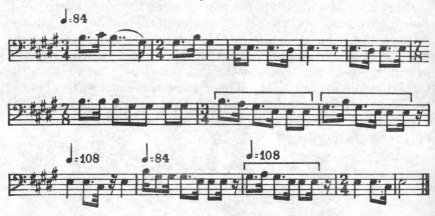

After the first performance of the Medicine Men's Dance, and at any time during the entire day, the men and women may perform any of the social dances except the Snake Dance (also called the Horned Owl Dance), which is given only in the fall, at the Hunting Dance. There is no prescribed order for these dances.

No. 16. Song of Medicine Men's Dance (b)
(Catalog No. 2173)

Recorded by BILLIE STEWART

No. 17. Song of Medicine Men's Dance (c)
(Catalog No. 2174)

Recorded by BILLIE STEWART

No. 18. Song of Medicine Men's Dance (d)

(Catalog No. 2175)

Recorded by BILLIE STEWART

CORN DANCE

A set of six Corn Dance songs was recorded by Billie Stewart, who composed them when he was a young man. These are sung at the beginning of the dance, the leader singing alone. This is different from the procedure in the Cypress Swamp group in which the leader sings one phrase of the song and then the dancers join in the singing. Billie Stewart leads this, as well as other dances in the Cow Creek group, and recorded all the songs of this series.

No. 19. Corn Dance Song (i)

(Catalog No. 2180)

No. 20. Corn Dance Song (j)

(Catalog No. 2181)

Fine

No. 21. Corn Dance Song (k)

(Catalog No. 2182)

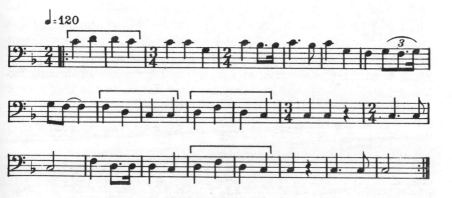

No. 22. Corn Dance Song (l)

(Catalog No. 2183)

Fine

No. 23. Corn Dance Song (m)

(Catalog No. 2184)

Fine

No. 24. Corn Dance Song (n)

(Catalog No. 2185)

CALUSA CORN DANCE

The Calusa Corn Dance song is very old, and the singer said it "came from the mountain men." On being questioned further, he said that the white people call those Indians the Calusa and that they spoke Spanish. Continuing, he said that long ago the Calusa and Seminole camped near one another and the people of each camp visited freely in the other, learning songs and joining in the dances. Later they fought, and the Seminole defeated the Calusa. In the Handbook of American Indians North of Mexico the Calusa are described as:

An important tribe of Florida, formerly holding the s.w. coast from about Tampa bay to C. Sable and C. Florida, together with all the outlying keys, and extending inland to L. Okeechobee. . . . The name, which cannot be interpreted, appears as Calos, or Carlos (province) in the early Spanish and French records, Caloosa and Coloosa in later English authors, and survives in Caloosa village, Caloosahatchee r., and Charlotte (for Carlos) harbor within their old territory. . . . Their history begins in 1513 when, with a fleet of 80 canoes they boldly attacked Ponce de León, who was about to land on their coast, and after an all-day fight compelled him to withdraw. Even at this early date they were already noted among the tribes for the golden wealth which they had accumulated from the numerous Spanish wrecks cast away upon the keys in passage from the s., and two centuries later they were regarded as veritable pirates, plundering and killing without mercy the crews of all vessels, excepting Span ish, so unfortunate as to be stranded in their neighborhood. In 1567 the Spaniards established a mission and fortified post among them, but both seem to have been discontinued soon after. . . . Romans states that in 1763, on the transfer of Florida from Spain to England the last remnant of the tribe, numbering then 80 families, or perhaps 350 souls, was removed to Havana. This, however, is only partially correct, as a considerable band under the name of Muspa Indians, or simply Spanish Indians, maintained their distinct existence and language in their ancient territory up to the close of the second Seminole war. . . . No vocabulary or other specimen of the language is known to exist beyond the town names and one or two other words given by Fontaneda, none of which afford basis for serious interpretation. [Mooney, 1907, pt. 1, pp. 195–196.]

A "confederacy or overlordship called the Calusa or Calos" is described by Swanton, who states that the group included "all of the Indians of southern Florida on the western side of the peninsula, from the Timucua territories as far as and including the Florida keys." This authority refers to two lists of Calusa towns, one in Fontaneda's Memoir and one in the Lowery manuscript and presents a combination of these lists (Swanton, 1922, pp. 330–332). The Calusa are mentioned in connection with the legendary origin of the ball game (cf. p. 186).

From this data it is possible to estimate the probable age of the Calusa songs, remembered by the Seminole. Other instances have been noted in which the age of an Indian song may be estimated by the time of tribal contacts or other events. Billie Stewart recorded seven Calusa songs of the Hunting Dance (Nos. 57–63).

ANALYSES OF CORN DANCE SONGS AND OF RELATED DANCES [10]

No. 1 (Cat. No. 2080).—A peculiarity of many Seminole songs is the use of an introduction (cf. p. 212). It was said that each sort of dance song had its own ending, and a similarity will be noted in the ending of the Buffalo Dance and Corn Dance songs. In some instances it is uncertain whether the closing tones of the transcription are part of the melody or a separate phrase. The singers were not encouraged to record the vocalizations that precede and follow many songs, as they are somewhat indefinite in length and a shortened form is sufficient for present purposes. Panther designated downward glissando progressions as "hollering" (cf. p. 214). The introduction to the present song is characterized by a descending fourth, and the song is based on two descending tetrachords.[11]

No. 2 (Cat. No. 2081).—The first phrase of this melody is based on a descending tetrachord. A minor third is prominent in the second portion, and the formal ending follows the song without a break in the time.

---

[10] These analyses should be understood as an aid to the study of the melodies. Attention is directed only to the chief peculiarities of the songs. More detailed analyses have been submitted to the Bureau of American Ethnology, and a summary of the characteristics of the songs is presented on pp. 210–216. The terminology used in former analyses is continued with the Seminole songs, thus making possible a comparison of the songs on a similar basis. These songs were recorded by a Columbia gramophone with special recorders and a specially constructed horn. The speed of the apparatus when recording the songs and when playing them for transcription was 160 revolutions a minute.

[11] Throughout these analyses the term "tetrachord" is applied to the interval of a perfect fourth with one or two intervening tones.

No. 25. Calusa Corn Dance Song

(Catalog No. 2064)

Recorded by BILLIE STEWART

No. 3 (Cat. No. 2082).—In this, as in the two preceding songs, the first tone is the highest tone of the compass, which is somewhat unusual in Indian songs. In its opening measure and general trend this resembles the two preceding songs, but the lowest tone of the tetrachord descends to E in the third measure, completing a major triad. A triplet of eighth notes occurs on a different count in each of the three opening measures. The accents were clearly given and the measure lengths are spaced accordingly. The interval of a fourth is less prominent than in the preceding songs, 16 of the 22 intervals being whole tones.

No. 4 (Cat. No. 2083).—The only tones in this song are those of the minor triad and fourth. A long phrase is indicated as the rhythmic unit. By comparing this phrase with the first ending we note a contraction of two double measures into one measure in triple time. As in the other Buffalo Dance songs, the formal ending begins on B flat.

No. 5 (Cat. No. 2084).—The first portion of this melody is minor in tonality and consists of two parts with a connective phrase. A descending tetrachord forms the framework of the first portion which has a compass of 11 tones and is major in tonality. The entire compass is reached by two intervals in the ninth measure. The second portion is minor in tonality, with the same keynote, and is different in both rhythm and melodic structure. By an ascending interval at the close, the song ends on the tone above the keynote. The intonation is good throughout the renditions and the time, including the 3-8 measures, is well sustained.

No. 6 (Cat. No. 2085).—This melody is characterized by descending fourths and whole tones; alternating ascending and descending semitones also occur frequently. Although the phrases are short and the count divisions simple, there is no rhythmic unit in the song.

No. 7 (Cat. No. 2086).—The framework of this melody consists of a minor triad and minor seventh (A–C–E–G) with the tones in descending order, as generally occurs in songs with this structure. The tone C is prominent and the major triad occurs in the fourth and other measures. The song is classified as major in tonality with C as the keynote. The form of the melody is unusually complicated, the rhythmic unit alternating with measures of various lengths. Attention is directed to the eleventh and twelfth measures from the close of the transcription, in which the rhythmic unit is elaborated. The short rests and prolonged tones were given clearly throughout the performance.

No. 8 (Cat. No. 2087).—The structure of this song consists of three periods, designated as A, B, and C (cf. p. xxiv). The singer said the first period of the song could be extended but that the second period was never changed. This is in accordance with the custom of other tribes, in songs with this structure. It is a lively melody but contains no rhythmic unit. The second above the keynote was uniformly raised a semitone. The song is major in tonality and based on a major triad with the keynote in the middle of the compass.

No. 9 (Cat. No. 2088).—Like the preceding song, this consists of three periods, designated as A, B, and C. As in other songs with this structure, the first period is the longest. The song is major in tonality and contains all the tones of the octave with the seventh lowered a semitone in every occurrence. The melody lies partly above and partly below the keynote. Two rhythmic units occur, the eighth notes that are unaccented in the first unit being accented in the second unit.

No. 10 (Cat. No. 2089).—This and the two songs following next are in period formation. As in No. 8, the second period is on the same pitch level as the first. In songs with this formation in tribes previously studied the second period has been higher in pitch level than the first. A major triad forms the framework of the melody with the fourth and sixth as passing tones. Although the rhythm is varied, the song contains no rhythmic unit.

No. 11 (Cat. No. 2090).—The rhythmic unit of this song is short and the melody contains many variants of this simple phrase, suggesting a freedom in repetition (cf. p. 215). A peculiarity of the melody is the frequent descent from the keynote to the seventh followed by a rest. This trailing of the voice is unusual in recorded Indian songs. The principal interval is a major third. After singing the song as transcribed the singer repeated the first period.

No. 12 (Cat. No. 2091).—This song is major in tonality and contains all the tones of the octave. Part of the melody lies above and part below the keynote, as in many Seminole songs. The principal intervals are major thirds and whole tones, which is unusual in the present series. The song is in period formation and contains an interesting rhythmic unit. After singing the song as transcribed, the singer repeated the first period.

No. 13 (Cat. No. 2384).—The following songs of the Buffalo Dance in the Cow Creek group are shorter than those of the Cypress Swamp group. The rhythmic unit of this song is short and the divisions of its unaccented count occur on the accented count of the fourth and eight measures. It is essentially a dancing song, with a smooth, even motion. A dotted note does not occur in the melody. The next Buffalo Dance song recorded by the same singer (not transcribed) contained the peculiar action of "swallowing the tone" mentioned on page 215. The rhythm of the accompanying coconut shell rattle was demonstrated and was in triple rhythm, two strokes of the rattle being followed by a rest.

No. 14 (Cat. No. 2317).—This resembles the song next preceding in the use of eighth and sixteenth notes but their order is reversed, the sixteenth notes preceding the eighths. This song has a smaller compass than the preceding. The first portion is based on the interval of a fourth and the second portion on the interval of a major third.

No. 15 (Cat. No. 2172).—The rhythm of this song is an interesting example of thematic treatment. The first, second, and fifth measures of the song begin with the same count division as the rhythmic unit, followed by a variety of rhythms. The same count division occurs on the unaccented count of the second and fourth measures from the close of the song. The harmonic structure of the melody is clear and the tonic triad [12] is emphasized but the use of the minor third below the keynote forms a minor triad and minor seventh, as in No. 9, these tones occurring in descending progression in the eighth and ninth measures.

No. 16 (Cat. No. 2173).—This melody comprises the tones of a major triad with the fourth as a passing tone in the second measure. A triplet of eighth notes is unaccented in the rhythmic unit and accented in two other measures of the song.

No. 17 (Cat. No. 2174).—This song contains only the tones of a major triad except the initial tone which is unaccented. About one-half of the intervals are major thirds, the semitones being next in frequency.

No. 18 (Cat. No. 2175).—The first portion of this song resembles rapid speech rather than singing. In this portion the words are heard while the remainder of the singing consists of vocables and syllables that may be one or two short words. After the change of tempo the rhythm is a typical dance rhythm with a short rhythmic unit and frequent changes of measure lengths. Except for D in the opening measure the tone material consists of a minor triad and fourth.

No. 19 (Cat. No. 2180).—Aside from the change of tempo, the principal interest in this song is in the fourth and sixth measures. The former reverses the count divisions of the rhythmic unit and the latter changes the rhythm of the first count of the unit. The tone material is that of the fourth 5-toned scale (cf. p. 210). Several renditions were recorded, the closing tone of the final rendition being followed by a close similar to that transcribed with Nos. 2, 3, and 4.

No. 20 (Cat. No. 2181).—The keynote implied by the sequence of tones in this song is F and the tone material is that of the first 5-toned scale in which the third and seventh tones do not occur (cf. p. 210). The small count divisions give distinction to this melody and were accurately repeated in all the renditions.

---

[12] This refers to the keynote of the song with its third and fifth.

No. 21 (Cat. No. 2182).—The tone material of this song is the first 5-toned scale, as in the song next preceding. The most prominent interval is a fourth enclosed within a fifth. These fifths, which occur in descending progression, are D–G, C–F, and G–C. The song has a compass of nine tones and a steadily descending trend. Three renditions were recorded, the transcription being from the first rendition.

No. 22 (Cat. No. 2183).—This pleasing melody was sung a semitone higher than the transcription. It contains a simple rhythmic unit and is based on the fourth 5-toned scale. Attention is directed to the vigorous phrase beginning in the fifth measure and introducing a change of rhythm. The framework consists of a descending major triad followed by the descending triad of the relative minor. The song closes with repetitions of a minor third.

No. 23 (Cat. No. 2184).—This song is framed on three descending intervals of a fourth, these being D–A and C–G followed by D–A in the lower octave. A rhythmic unit occurs three times and the song did not vary in its repetitions. The rendition was a semitone higher than the transcription.

No. 24 (Cat. No. 2185).—This song opens with an incomplete rhythmic unit. The initial tones of this unit may have been omitted accidentally. The sequence of tones suggests F as the keynote though it occurs only as a short, unaccented tone. The rendition was a semitone higher than the transcription.

No. 25 (Cat. No. 2064).—This is the only song recorded by Billie Stewart which has the period formation, and is a song of the Calusa. The period formation occurred in a majority of the Corn Dance songs recorded by Panther, of the Cypress Swamp group, and we note that the Calusa formerly lived south of the Cow Creek Seminole. In this song the first period occurs six times and the second period occurs only once. No two occurrences of the first period are alike, though the principal tones and general pattern of the melody are the same. The transcription is from the first rendition of the song. A second rendition contains other variations of the first period, while the second period is repeated with accuracy. A slight extension of the first period has been noted with songs of this formation in other tribes but this is so extensive as to suggest an improvisation. It was noted as a custom among the Choctaw (Densmore, 1943 b). The second period of this song is in a more rapid tempo than the first, which is a characteristic of the form. The most frequent interval is a major third, with the fourth next in number of occurrences. The labial m was sung clearly in all renditions (cf. p. 213). It occurs also in Nos. 103 and 237.

HUNTING DANCE

The second gathering of the Seminole is the Hunting Dance which is held in October, its purpose being to secure success on the hunt. It resembles the Corn Dance in its ceremonial aspect, and numerous social dances are held, as on that occasion. The Snake Dance, also called the Horned Owl Dance, is given only at the Hunting Dance, but it appears that the other social dances here described may be given at either time. According to Mrs. Minnie Moore Willson, the Hunting Dance is held every 4 years.[13] The present informants did not state the frequency of the dance.

The principal animals hunted by the Seminole are the alligator, deer, bear, turkey, raccoon, and bobcat. The extent of their hunting is shown by the following statement, made in 1931: "Thirty years ago it was an annual event for 20 or 25 canoes loaded with Seminoles, their pigs, chickens, children, and the pelts from a year's hunting, to glide down the North New River and tie up to the trading post of Frank Stranahan in Fort Lauderdale" (Nash, 1931, p. 49).[14]

CYPRESS SWAMP GROUP

The songs of the Hunting Dance in the Cypress Swamp group were recorded by Charlie Billie, who is leader of that dance as well as of the Corn Dance (1931). In the Hunting Dance the custom differs from the Corn Dance in that only the leader and his helper sing, the people not joining with them. The opening songs of this series are probably ceremonial, but the third appears to be a variant of a Bird Dance song (No. 83) which was recorded by Panther. When recording the songs of the Corn Dance (not transcribed) Charlie Billie said that the first four songs were ceremonial and the fifth was the song of an incidental social dance.

---

[13] "This festival occurs only in cycles—once every four years—and the character of its observance is known to but few, if any, white people" (Willson, 1910, p. 100). Mrs. Willson attended this dance and describes it, with a diagram, on pp. 100–106 of her book.

[14] Frank Stranahan is mentioned also in connection with mortuary customs on page 36 of this report, and his wife gave interesting information on other subjects (pp. 20, 26, 36, 37).

No. 26. Cypress Swamp Hunting Dance Song (a)
(Catalog No. 2072)

Fine

No. 27. Cypress Swamp Hunting Dance Song (b)
(Catalog No. 2073)

No. 28. Cypress Swamp Hunting Dance Song (c)
(Catalog No. 2074)

No. 29. Cypress Swamp Hunting Dance Song (d)
(Catalog No. 2075)

No. 30. Cypress Swamp Hunting Dance Song (e)
(Catalog No. 2076)

No. 31. Cypress Swamp Hunting Dance Song (f)
(Catalog No. 2077)

No. 32. Cypress Swamp Hunting Dance Song (g)
(Catalog No. 2078)

No. 33. Cypress Swamp Hunting Dance Song (h)

(Catalog No. 2079)

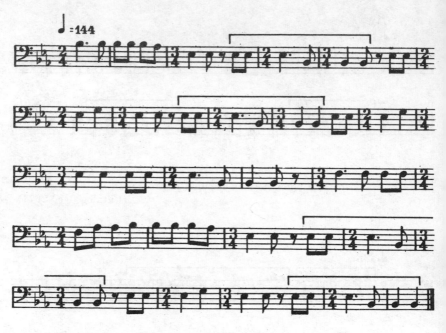

COW CREEK GROUP

The Hunting Dance songs of the Cow Creek group were recorded by Billie Stewart, who is the leader of that dance in the group. He speaks only fragmentary English and an interpreter was not available, but he consulted often with his friend Charlie Snow, who is familiar with the dance and has a better use of English. They invited the writer and her sister to attend the Hunting Dance the next autumn but it was impossible to accept the invitation.

The Medicine Men's Dance is held before the Hunting Dance, as before the Corn Dance, but at this time it is not preceded by entrance into the sweat lodge. The ceremonial songs used in this dance are probably those recorded by the same singer and presented in connection with the Corn Dance (Nos. 15–18).

These informants stated that the dancers in the Hunting Dance form in a long line, led by a man with a coconut shell rattle, and that the dancers join him in singing the songs. In describing the Hunting Dance of the Cypress Swamp group, Charlie Billie said that the leader and his helper sang the songs. It will be noted that the dancers among the Seminole do not sing, the exceptions in the present series being the Screech Owl and Snake dances in which it was said that both men and women danced and that only the men sang, and the Chicken Dance and Cow Creek Hunting Dance in which all the dancers join.

In the Hunting Dance the movements of the dancers are outlined by four posts, at the corners of a square. A fire is in the middle of this space. The dancers start at the west and move toward the south, then east, and then north; the remainder of the evolutions are around the four posts, in a definite order. Billie Stewart sketched the movement of his dance and did it so rapidly that he was asked to sketch it again for comparison. The sketches showed the same outline. Passing by the southwest and southeast posts the dancers encircled the northeast post, approaching it from the east. Then they circled the southwest post, and went to the northwest post, moving around it and returning to the east side of the square where they passed around the southeast post, after which they went north, passed around the outline of the square and returned to their original position. Stewart said that each song is sung "about four times," then the "howls" or glissando cries are given and the next song is begun without a pause.

All the songs of this series were recorded, as stated, by Billie Stewart.

No. 34. Cow Creek Hunting Dance Song (a)
(Catalog No. 2149)

Fine

No. 35. Cow Creek Hunting Dance Song (b)
(Catalog No. 2150)

No. 36. Cow Creek Hunting Dance Song (c)
(Catalog No. 2151)

No. 37. Cow Creek Hunting Dance Song (d)
(Catalog No. 2152)

No. 38. Cow Creek Hunting Dance Song (e)
(Catalog No. 2153)

No. 39. Cow Creek Hunting Dance Song (f)
(Catalog No. 2154)

No. 40. Cow Creek Hunting Dance Song (g)

(Catalog No. 2155)

Fine

No. 41. Cow Creek Hunting Dance Song (h)

(Catalog No. 2156)

Fine

No. 42. Cow Creek Hunting Dance Song (i)

(Catalog No. 2157)

No. 42. Cow Creek Hunting Dance Song (i)—Continued

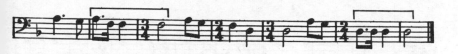

No. 43. Cow Creek Hunting Dance Song (j)

(Catalog No. 2158)

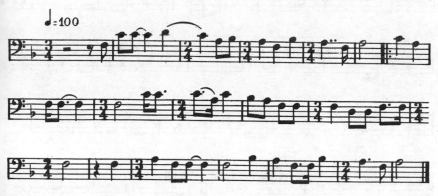

No. 44. Cow Creek Hunting Dance Song (k)

(Catalog No. 2159)

Fine

No. 45. Cow Creek Hunting Dance Song (l)
(Catalog No. 2160)

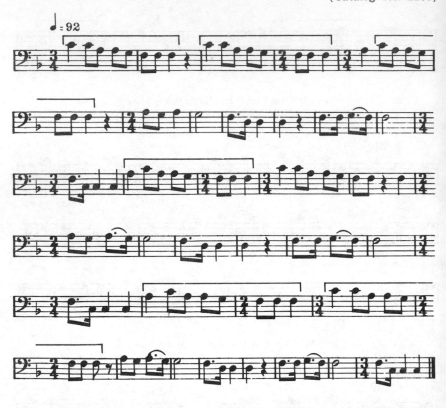

No. 46. Cow Creek Hunting Dance Song (m)
(Catalog No. 2161)

No. 47. Cow Creek Hunting Dance Song (n)

(Catalog No. 2162)

No. 48. Cow Creek Hunting Dance Song (o)

(Catalog No. 2163)

No. 49. Cow Creek Hunting Dance Song (p)
(Catalog No. 2164)

Fine

No. 50. Cow Creek Hunting Dance Song (q)
(Catalog No. 2165)

No. 51. Cow Creek Hunting Dance Song (r)
(Catalog No. 2166)

No. 52. Cow Creek Hunting Dance Song (s)

(Catalog No. 2167)

Fine

No. 53. Cow Creek Hunting Dance Song (t)

(Catalog No. 2168)

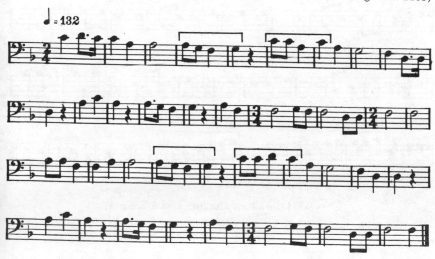

No. 54. Cow Creek Hunting Dance Song (u)

(Catalog No. 2169)

No. 55. Cow Creek Hunting Dance Song (v)

(Catalog No. 2170)

No. 55. Cow Creek Hunting Dance Song (v)—Continued

No. 56. Cow Creek Hunting Dance Song (w)

(Catalog No. 2171)

CALUSA HUNTING DANCE

Billie Stewart recorded the seven Calusa songs of the Hunting Dance.

No. 57. Calusa Hunting Dance Song (a)

(Catalog No. 2065)

No. 58. Calusa Hunting Dance Song (b)

(Catalog No. 2066)

No. 59. Calusa Hunting Dance Song (c)

(Catalog No. 2067)

No. 60. Calusa Hunting Dance Song (d)

(Catalog No. 2068)

338460 O—56——8

No. 61. Calusa Hunting Dance Song (e)

(Catalog No. 2069)

No. 62. Calusa Hunting Dance Song (f)

(Catalog No. 2070)

Fine

No. 63. Calusa Hunting Dance Song (g)

(Catalog No. 2071)

No. 63. Calusa Hunting Dance Song (g)—Continued

ANALYSES OF HUNTING DANCE SONGS

CYPRESS SWAMP GROUP

No. 26 (Cat. No. 2072).—This and the seven songs next following were recorded by Charlie Billie. Attention is directed to the similarity in tempo and pitch of these songs, half having E flat and half having F as a keynote, while the meter in six of the songs is ♩=138 or ♩=144. This is the more interesting, as the songs were recorded under difficult circumstances, in the evening, with many onlookers. The tones of the present melody consist chiefly of two overlapping triads, the upper being major and the lower being minor. Together these constitute a minor triad with minor seventh, a framework noted first in No. 9. As in other songs with this melodic formation, the tones occur in downward progression. The performance was followed by the glissando tones that characterize Seminole dance songs. These were not transcribed.

No. 27 (Cat. No. 2073).—This melody does not have the steadily descending trend of the preceding song but the descending intervals are more in number than the ascending intervals. A simple phrase, indicated as a rhythmic unit, occurs three times in the song which contains only the tones of a major triad.

No. 28 (Cat. No. 2074).—This melody is much larger in compass and more active in movement than the preceding songs. It contains 2 ascending sevenths, 2 ascending sixths, and 14 intervals of a fourth. The fourth above the keynote is used effectively and, in its first occurrence, is approached by an ascending seventh.

No. 29 (Cat. No. 2075).—A short rhythmic unit marks a difference between this and the preceding songs of the group. This unit occurs only on the tones F–C. The song contains only the tones of a major triad and second but shows an interesting variety of intervals.

No. 30 (Cat. No. 2076).—The first, second, and third measures of this song, with their free melodic movement, seem to be an introduction to the melody which is less interesting than a majority of Seminole songs. Except for one tone the song is based on a major triad and fourth, the latter occurring as a passing tone.

No. 31 (Cat. No. 2077).—The framework and compass of this is the same as the preceding song but the only tones are those of a major triad. The rhythm is more varied and the rhythmic unit occurs more frequently. This melody is better suited for dancing, and the succession of ascending and descending intervals suggests the motion of the dancers. The same characteristic occurs in several other dancing songs of this series.

No. 32 (Cat. No. 2078).—The metric unit of this song is designated as an eighth note, each measure being clearly sung in this meter. A variety of progressions occur, including minor sixths, fifths, and minor seconds. It is a pleasing melody, major in tonality and containing all the tones of the octave except the second and seventh.

No. 33 (Cat. No. 2079).—Like many Seminole songs, this melody lies partly above and partly below the keynote. It opens with a descent of an octave in three measures, followed by a long, gradual return to the highest tone, after which it descends to the lowest tone in three measures. The closing measures are based on the interval of a fourth, the song ending on the lowest tone of its compass. The interval of a fourth comprises 10 of the 21 progressions. All the tones of the octave except the sixth and seventh are present in the melody.

COW CREEK GROUP

This series of 23 songs, recorded by Billie Stewart, contains a similarity in general structure. Fifteen of these songs begin on C or have C as the first accented tone. Seventeen are based on the major triad on F, and six have E or E-flat as the keynote. Apart from these general resemblances, the songs have different peculiarities that are noted briefly. They show the ability of the Indian to diversify simple material in melody and rhythm.

No. 34 (Cat. No. 2149).—The first half of this melody is based on two descending triads, C–A–F and G–E–C. The second and third portions are based on the tonic triad with the seventh as an accented tone. All the tones of the octave are present in the song.

No. 35 (Cat. No. 2150).—The triad F–A–C forms the framework of this melody which lies partly above and partly below the keynote. Its chief interest lies in the ascending seventh and change of tempo at the beginning of the second period.

No. 36 (Cat. No. 2151).—Although it is slow in tempo, this melody is so clear and simple in rhythm that it appears to be a lively song. The initial intervals are the same as in a majority of the songs in this series and the melody is based in a major triad, with special prominence of the fourth above the keynote.

No. 37 (Cat. No. 2152).—The familiar opening on D and C occurs in this song which begins on the accented count of the measure. The melody has a compass of nine tones and progresses chiefly by whole tones. The third, fourth, and fifth measures would constitute an occurrence of the rhythmic unit except for the short rest which divides the phrase. By this rest, the tones C–G become the end of the preceding phrase. The descending tetrachords C–A–G, G–F–D, and C–B-flat–G are prominent in the melody. A repetition of the song ended in the middle of the fourth measure and was followed by the glissando ending. The Seminole, more than northern tribes, are willing to conclude a song before reaching the end of the melody. In some dances the singing ends when the dancers have completed a circle and returned to the east, thus they are accustomed to incomplete renditions of a song.

No. 38 (Cat. No. 2153).—A slower tempo and lower keynote mark this melody which begins with the descending whole tone noted in many other songs of the series. The intervals include five semitones which is an unusually large number of this interval. All the tones of the octave are present except the second.

No. 39 (Cat. No. 2154).—This interesting melody is based on the descending tetrachord B–A–F-sharp, followed by E and the descending fourth E–B, with a return to the keynote. The tempo is slow but the effect is lively, especially in the portion beginning with the fourth measure.

No. 40 (Cat. No. 2155).—A short rhythmic unit occurs frequently in this song which is lively in character. The rhythm of the song as a whole is worthy of attention. The rhythmic unit opens the melody, followed by a freely melodic phrase with several descending intervals and an ascending fourth. The latter part of the song contains repetitions of the rhythmic unit on four successive descending tones, followed by an ascent of a fourth to the keynote.

No. 41 (Cat. No. 2156).—With a small compass of five tones, this song is distinctly harmonic in structure. The rhythmic unit is long and interesting.

No. 42 (Cat. No. 2157).—The framework of this melody consists of two overlapping triads constituting a minor triad with minor seventh. The compass of the song is comprised within these seven tones and progression is chiefly by fourths and whole tones.

No. 43 (Cat. No. 2158).—About two-thirds of this melody is framed on the descending triad C–A–F, this being followed by C–A–F–D, completing a minor triad and minor seventh, with B-flat as a passing tone. The song closes on the tetrachord B-flat–A–F. The rhythm has a long swing but no unit. Prolonged tones and a downward gliding of the voice on a portion of the intervals characterize this melody.

No. 44 (Cat. No. 2159).—In this song we find the descending triads C–A–F and A–F–D which characterized the two songs next preceding but the emphasis on the major triad is stronger than in the preceding songs. The phrase in the sixth measure is not regarded as a rhythmic unit as in its two other occurrences it forms part of a longer phrase. The principal intervals are major thirds and semitones which is a somewhat unusual combination of intervals. The semitones occur between A and B-flat, and are usually in descending progression. This was followed by a song which was not transcribed because it differed from the present melody only in unimportant note-values. The singer's attention was called to this when the songs were recorded and he replied, as in other instances, "Almost same, but different song."

No. 45 (Cat. No. 2160).—A short, descending phrase on the tonic triad forms the rhythmic unit of this song. After repetitions of this unit the descending minor triad A–F–D is introduced. This is more pleasing than a majority of melodies based on these triads. The one material is that of the fourth 5-toned scale and more than half the intervals are whole tones.

No. 46 (Cat. No. 2161).—The overlapping triads noted in the preceding song are also present in this melody but the tonality is minor. The tempo is much slower than in the preceding song. An interesting break in the rhythm occurs in the fifth measure.

No. 47 (Cat. No. 2162). The only tones in this melody are those of the minor triad and minor seventh, with one occurrence of B-flat as a passing tone. The song is classified as major in tonality. The rests before D and F in the closing measures are interesting and effective.

No. 48 (Cat. No. 2163).—About half the intervals in this song are semitones which the Indian always sings with some uncertainty. The pitch of the tone transcribed as B-flat is maintained with reasonable accuracy but the tone transcribed as A is variable. The interval between E and F is also uncertain and the transcription indicates the pitch as nearly as possible. The principal interest of the song lies in the two rhythmic units which seem to answer one another. The melody is lively and the rest near the close is effective, the repetition of the song following without a pause. The second and sixth above the keynote do not appear in the melody which is major in tonality.

No. 49 (Cat. No. 2164).—Like the song next preceding, this melody begins with an ascending fifth and descends to F by the tones B-flat and A. The former melody returned to A but this song ascends to B-flat which is strongly emphasized throughout the remainder of the melody. The semitone is the most frequent interval and was sung with more distinctness than in the song next preceding. The compass is only five tones, the song beginning and ending on the lowest tone of the compass.

No. 50 (Cat. No. 2165).—The rhythmic structure of this song consists of three periods, each containing five measures. The rest in the fourth from the final measure gives variety to the rhythm. In melodic material the song is simple, being based on the tonic triad with the second and seventh as unimportant tones. Two renditions were recorded without a pause.

No. 51 (Cat. No. 2166).—This song is minor in tonality and has a compass of seven tones. The principal intervals are whole tones and minor thirds. The sequence of tones in the rhythmic unit produces two descending tetrachords, C–B-flat–G and B-flat–G–F.

No. 52 (Cat. No. 2167).—Except for the tones in the closing measures this song is based entirely on the tonic triad and fourth, with the latter as a prominent tone. The most frequent interval is a semitone, next in frequency being a major third.

No. 53 (Cat. No. 2168).—An ascending interval at the close of a phrase characterizes this song. The melody opens with two phrases, each containing five measures. These are followed by short, exclamatory phrases, after which the five-measure phrases continue to the close of the song. Attention is directed to the measure in triple time occurring about halfway through the song which varies the rhythm and gives it stability. The tone material is that of the fourth 5-toned scale.

No. 54 (Cat. No. 2169).—A phrase containing five measures occurs throughout this melody and characterizes the preceding song. The rhythmic units are short and descending in trend. The triple measure before the final phrase resembles the second rhythmic unit and the variation adds to the interest of the rhythm.   The melody is major in tonality and progresses chiefly by major thirds and whole tones.

No. 55 (Cat. No. 2170).—In this song we find a series of rapidly descending progressions which is unusual in Indian songs.   The compass of each series is a fifth, the series occurring first from B-flat to E-flat and then from C to F.

No. 56 (Cat. No. 2171).—The keynote is next to the highest tone in this song and is prominent throughout the melody, though it does not occur on the accented portion of a measure.   The song is based chiefly on three descending tetrachords.   The opening portion is on the tetrachord G–B-flat C, the tones occurring in both ascending and descending progression.   The overlapping descending tetrachord B-flat–G–F appears in the third measure.   The third tetrachord is also descending and consists of the tones G–F–D, continuing for several measures.   The tones are those of the fourth 5-toned scale and the intervals consist of minor thirds and whole tones.

CALUSA HUNTING DANCE

No. 57 (Cat. No. 2065).—The phrase transcribed as an introduction to this song was given after, as well as before, many of the hunting songs recorded by this singer.   It is not considered necessary to present it in each instance.   The compass and general trend of this melody are the same as in the Calusa Corn dance song (No. 25) but the character of the melody is entirely different.   The phrase in double time that occurs midway through the song gives stability to the rhythm of the melody as a whole.   A similar rhythm occurs in the closing measures.

No. 58 (Cat. No. 2066).—This resembles the song next preceding in general trend but the compass is larger and the rhythm is more elaborate.   The opening interval is the same, but C occurs on an unaccented instead of the accented portion of the measure.   The tempo changes frequently and the original tempo returns at the close of the song with a repetition of the rhythmic unit in which quarter notes are substituted for eighth notes.   The tone transcribed as D-flat is effective and was clearly sung.

No. 59 (Cat. No. 2067).—Prolonged tones characterize this melody and occur in the rhythmic unit.   The compass comprises 10 tones and the song contains all the tones of the octave except the sixth.   With three exceptions the accented tones are those of the tonic triad.

No. 60 (Cat. No. 2068).—The trend of this melody consists of short, descending phrases.   Consecutive fourths occur in ascending and descending progression in the middle and latter part of the song.   The tone material is that of the second 5-toned scale, with the fourth as a prominent tone.   The seventh measure· from the close of the song contains the same phrase as the rhythmic unit but accented differently.

Such changes of accent give variety to Indian melodies and are an interesting phase of thematic treatment.

No. 61 (Cat. No. 2069).—In its opening tones this song is similar to several others in the series, and the same tones continue during five measures. The transfer of accent from C to D in the third measure is interesting. The sixth, seventh, and eighth measures are based on descending fourths and tetrachords which occur consecutively in the eighth measure. The remainder of the melody is based on the tonic triad. The tempo is slower than is customary in Seminole songs. Attention is directed to a comparison between the rhythm of the fourth and fifth measures and that of the closing measures of the song.

No. 62 (Cat. No. 2070).—Attention is directed to a comparison between the opening measures of this song and the phrase which follows *Fine.* It will be noted that the changes of tempo are the same in both phrases, and that the melody of the first is condensed in the second phrase. The song is based on the first 5-toned scale and two-thirds of the progressions are whole tones.

No. 63 (Cat. No. 2071).—This transcription consists of three sections, each more lively than the preceding. It was said to be one song but Indians frequently fail to distinguish between a song and a set of songs that are called "one *singing.*" This singer spoke and understood little English and the work was done without a competent interpreter. Thus it is possible that the performance may be three songs that were sung consecutively. When recorded, each section was followed by the glissando phrases that usually end Seminole songs and are used with considerable freedom. The second section was sung four times. The third section is characterized by a short, descending phrase with a compass of five tones. Two tetrachords enclosed within a fifth occur in the third measure of this section, and a tetrachord within a fifth occurs in the following measure. These two measures recur near the end of the melody.

SOCIAL DANCES

ALLIGATOR DANCE

The social dances given at the time of the Corn and Hunting Dances are very old and are generally connected with birds and animals. Panther said, "A long time ago all the animals talked like people. The alligators made up this dance at that time. There is an old story that when the people all die maybe the animals will come back again as they were before, talking like people." The Alligator Dance is the most important of these incidental dances and was given at night. Its songs were recorded by the leaders in both the Cypress Swamp and Cow Creek groups.

A line of dances led by a man at the right is shown in plate 17, *a*. The name of this dance was not determined.

CYPRESS SWAMP GROUP

Panther described the Alligator Dance as given by his group and said the songs are sung by a man with a coconut shell rattle who walks at the head of the line of dancers. Men and women walk in couples and follow the leader around the fire. As they walk, he sings a song without shaking the rattle, then there is a change in the music and the motion. The leader shakes his rattle, the people shout *ho ho ho* in rhythm and each couple dances alone, holding hands. Each couple "dances round and round" until a signal is given, then they walk forward as before, the leader singing without shaking the rattle. There is no prescribed order for the songs and many persons take part in the dance. The meaning of the words in the next song was not given, and it is probable the words are obsolete and the meaning unknown. Four songs were recorded by Panther, but only two were transcribed. The melody of the last two was practically the same as that of the first of the songs here presented, but there was no increase in the tempo, as in this song .

No. 64. Alligator Dance Song (a)

(Catalog No. 2122)

Recorded by PANTHER

No. 65. Alligator Dance Song (b)

(Catalog No. 2123)

Recorded by PANTHER

The closing song of this dance as given in the Everglades was also recorded.

No. 66. Closing Song of Alligator Dance

(Catalog No. 2124)

Recorded by PANTHER

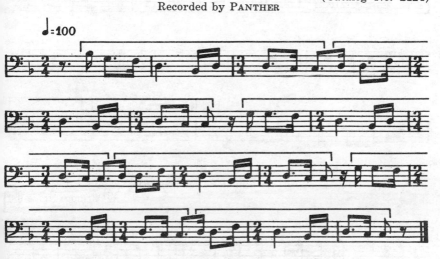

COW CREEK GROUP

The songs next following are those of the same dance in the Cow Creek group. No mention was made of a difference in the motion of the dance, and the leader in this, as in other dances, was Billie Stewart, who recorded all the songs of the dance.

No. 67. Alligator Dance Song (c)

(Catalog No. 2298)

No. 68. Alligator Dance Song (d)

(Catalog No. 2299)

No. 69. Alligator Dance Song (e)

(Catalog No. 2300)

No. 70. Alligator Dance Song (f)

(Catalog No. 2301)

Fine

No. 71. Alligator Dance Song (g)

(Catalog No. 2302)

No. 72. Alligator Dance Song (h)

(Catalog No. 2303)

No. 73. Alligator Dance Song (i)

(Catalog No. 2304)

Fine

BABY ALLIGATOR DANCE

No information was obtained concerning the Baby Alligator Dance except that it was performed by men and women at the Corn Dance or at any time during the summer.

No. 74. Baby Alligator Dance Song (a)

(Catalog No. 2442)

Recorded by BILLIE STEWART

No. 75. Baby Alligator Dance Song (b)

(Catalog No. 2443)

Recorded by BILLIE STEWART

LIZARD DANCE

In the Lizard Dance men and women alternate, but do not hold hands. A man with a coconut-shell rattle sings, standing still. The dancers do not join in the songs.

No. 76. Lizard Dance Song (a)

Recorded by BILLIE STEWART

(Catalog No. 2440)

No. 77. Lizard Dance Song (b)

Recorded by BILLIE STEWART

(Catalog No. 2441)

Shouts

BIRD DANCES—CYPRESS SWAMP GROUP

The Ibis and Egret are among the most prominent dances given at a Corn Dance, and Panther included them in the general designation of Bird Dances. These are performed only in the daytime, and the men wear feathers of all sorts in their turbans and carry poles with gay feathers at the end. Only men and boys take part in these dances, and they are led by two men, dancing side by side and having a coconut shell rattle in each hand. At the rear of the dancers are two old men of the Bird clan who push the dancers along and keep the company together. The songs of dances are said to be very old. If words occur, their meaning has been forgotten but the syllables are repeated by rote. The songs are short and are in sets of four. After each set the dancers stand in their places during a pause. These songs are presented in the order in which they were recorded, and no attempt has been made to separate them into sets of four. Their peculiar ending is described on page 214.

All the Bird Dance songs were recorded by Panther.

No. 78. Bird Dance Song (a)

(Catalog No. 2092)

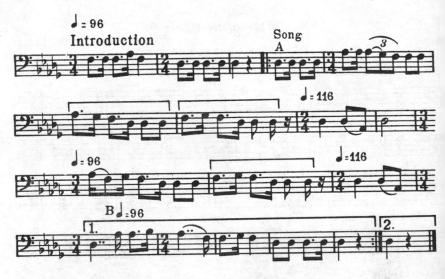

No. 79. Bird Dance Song (b)

(Catalog No. 2093)

No. 80. Bird Dance Song (c)

(Catalog No. 2094)

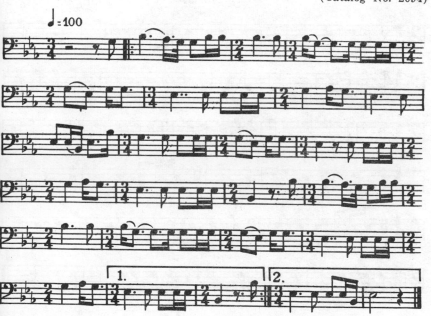

No. 81. Bird Dance Song (d)

(Catalog No. 2095)

No. 82. Bird Dance Song (e)

(Catalog No. 2096)

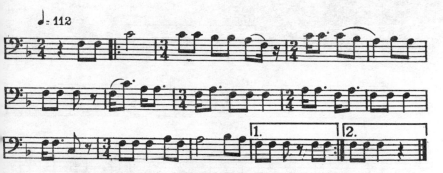

No. 83. Bird Dance Song (f)

(Catalog No. 2097)

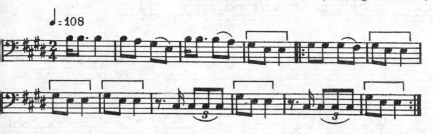

No. 84. Bird Dance Song (g)

(Catalog No. 2098)

Fine

No. 85. Bird Dance Song (h)

(Catalog No. 2099)

No. 86. Bird Dance Song (i)

(Catalog No. 2100)

No. 87. Bird Dance Song (j)

(Catalog No. 2101)

No. 88. Bird Dance Song (k)

(Catalog No. 2102)

No. 89. Bird Dance Song (l)

(Catalog No. 2103)

No. 90. Bird Dance Song (m)

(Catalog No. 2104)

No. 91. Bird Dance Song (n)

(Catalog No. 2105)

CHICKEN DANCE

Six dances of the Seminole were imitations of the actions of birds and animals. The first of these is the Chicken Dance (Nos. 92–95), others are the Quail, Blackbird, Buzzard, and Catfish Dances, while the children have a dance in which they imitate a "little fish" (No. 201). It is possible that other dances contained such imitations but were not mentioned by the singers. This custom had been noted by the writer only among the Indians in Wisconsin and at Neah Bay, in northwest Washington. Six such dances were witnessed among the Menominee, and their songs were recorded (Densmore, 1932 a, pp. 188–194), and a smaller number were witnessed among the Winnebago and their songs were obtained (Densmore, MS.). The Makah at Neah Bay impersonated birds, animals, and a "little fish" in social dances, and the songs of these were recorded (Densmore 1939, pp. 119–128). Dances impersonating animals were presented at a dance at Neah Bay, attended by the writer.

One of the imitative dances given in the evenings during a Corn Dance is the Chicken Dance. Everyone joins in this dance and all who know the songs may join the singing, moving their arms in imitation of the fluttering wings of a domestic fowl. Five songs of this dance were recorded but only four are presented, the fifth song being practically the same as the fourth.

No. 92. Chicken Dance Song (a)

(Catalog No. 2188)

Recorded by BILLIE STEWART

No. 93. Chicken Dance Song (b)

(Catalog No. 2189)

Recorded by BILLIE STEWART

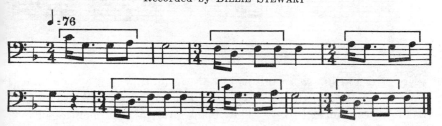

No. 94. Chicken Dance Song (c)

(Catalog No. 2190)

Recorded by BILLIE STEWART

No. 95. Chicken Dance Song (d)

Recorded by BILLIE STEWART

(Catalog No. 2191)

BLACK GRASS DANCE

No information was obtained concerning this dance, which was given at the time of the Corn Dance. The name may refer to an area that has been burned over. The "black prairie" was mentioned in a song recorded by Susie Tiger, but no connection with the "black grass" was mentioned.

No. 96. Black Grass Dance Song (a)

Recorded by BILLIE STEWART

(Catalog No. 2422)

No. 97. Black Grass Dance Song (b)

(Catalog No. 2423)

Recorded by BILLIE STEWART

No. 98. Black Grass Dance Song (c)

(Catalog No. 2424)

Recorded by BILLIE STEWART

STOMP DANCE

Among the Choctaw in Mississippi a Stomp Dance was witnessed in 1933 (Densmore, 1943 b, p. 160). The procedure differed somewhat from the description of the Seminole dance, given by Billie Stewart. Men and women took part in the Choctaw dance, standing in a circle, the leader of the singing being in the middle of the circle. The motion of the dance consisted in jumping up and down with both feet at once, the circle of dancers moving contraclockwise. No instrumental accompaniment was used with the songs.

Among the Seminole, the Stomp Dance is danced at night, during a Corn Dance. The singer is at one side of the line of dancers and beats on a "cypress-knee drum." The leader of the dancers has no instrument and the women have turtle-shell rattles (or small tin-can rattles) at the knee, as in the Corn Dance. Men and women alternate in the line of dancers, and the motion is "walking rapidly and heavily," this being "the same as for the dance in Oklahoma." Billie Stewart said he was taught that the Stomp Dance was "supposed to be like the Corn Dance" and that the Seminole received it from the Muskogee, but it was not a subject of inquiry. Six of its songs are presented, the second containing the words "I love the Stomp Dance, it should be continued always." The entire series was recorded by Billie Stewart.

No. 99. Stomp Dance Song (a)

(Catalog No. 2393)

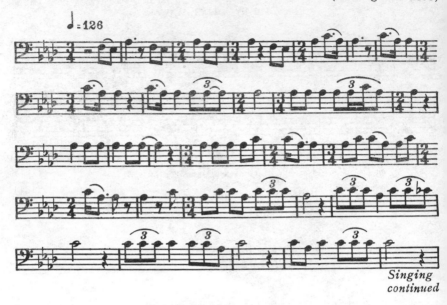

*Singing
continued*

No. 100. Stomp Dance Song (b)

(Catalog No. 2394)

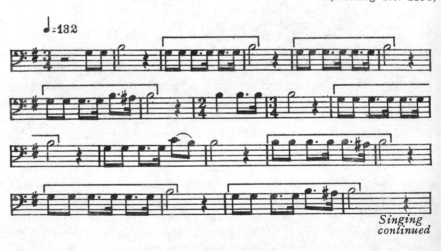

*Singing
continued*

No. 101. Stomp Dance Song (c)

(Catalog No. 2395)

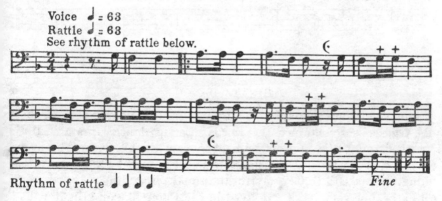

No. 102. Stomp Dance Song (d)

(Catalog No. 2396)

Voice ♩ = 63
Rattle ♩ = 63
See rhythm of rattle below.

Rhythm of rattle ♩ ♩ ♩ ♩   *Fine*

No. 103. Stomp Dance Song (e)

(Catalog No. 2397)

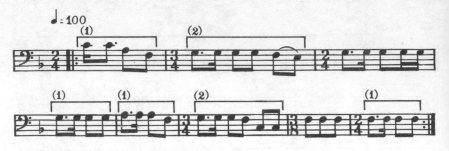

No. 104. Stomp Dance Song (f)

(Catalog No. 2398)

HINATA DANCE

This is an "outside dance," held during the Stomp Dance. A song not transcribed contained the words "Let us dance Hinata." Both Panther and Billie Stewart had taken part in this dance, the latter saying that he learned the dance when a boy and "liked it." The "hinata" was said to be a mythical animal resembling a lizard or an alligator, but very large. It lived in the water like an alligator, had a long tail, and killed people. Its abode was "farther north." Both men and women take part in the Hinata Dance, "alternating and moving in single file as in the Snake Dance, and led by the singer with a rattle." A change of motion is noted in connection with one group of songs, but the singer was too much occupied with recording the songs to be questioned closely concerning the motion of the dance.

All the songs of the Hinata Dance were recorded by Panther.

No. 105. Hinata Dance Song (a)

(Catalog No. 2399)

No. 106. Hinata Dance Song (b)

(Catalog No. 2400)

Shouts

No. 107. Hinata Dance Song (c)

(Catalog No. 2401)

No. 108. Hinata Dance Song (d)

(Catalog No. 2402)

No. 109. Hinata Dance Song (e)

(Catalog No. 2403)

No. 110. Hinata Dance Song (f)

(Catalog No. 2404)

No. 111. Hinata Dance Song (g)

(Catalog No. 2405)

No. 112. Hinata Dance Song (h)

(Catalog No. 2406)

The two songs next following constitute a group, the singer saying
"when the singer shakes his rattle the women go on dancing and the
men hop around the women, something like a kangaroo hopping."

No. 113. Hinata Dance Song (i)

(Catalog No. 2407)

No. 114. Hinata Dance Song (j)

(Catalog No. 2408)

The four songs next following are a "set," the singer stating that the first and second had words while the others had none. No translation of the words was obtained.

No. 115. Hinata Dance Song (k)

(Catalog No. 2409)

No. 116. Hinata Dance Song (l)

(Catalog No. 2410)

No. 117. Hinata Dance Song (m)

(Catalog No. 2411)

No. 118. Hinata Dance Song (n)

(Catalog No. 2412)

Three songs of a set of four Hinata Dance songs were transcribed, as follows.

No. 119. Hinata Dance Song (o)

(Catalog No. 2413)

No. 120. Hinata Dance Song (p)

(Catalog No. 2414)

No. 121. Hinata Dance Song (q)

(Catalog No. 2415)

Several other songs of this dance were recorded but not transcribed. The characteristics were similar to the songs which are presented.

QUAIL DANCE

Songs of the Quail Dance were recorded in both the Cypress Swamp and Cow Creek groups. Panther stated that in the former group the dancers circle about four times around the fire, pause and pretend to pick up food like a quail, then "reverse" and circle the fire in the opposite direction. He said "they make the four dancings with this one song." The song is in two sections and Panther paused between them when recording. The first portion is sung when the dancers pretend to pick up food, like a quail, and the second portion while they are dancing. The changes of tempo probably correspond to the action of the dancers. These songs were accompanied, in the dance, by the shaking of a coconut shell rattle.

No. 122. Quail Dance Song (a)

Recorded by PANTHER

(Catalog No. 2131)

Two songs of the Quail dance in the Cow Creek group were recorded by Billie Stewart but only one is presented.

No. 123. Quail Dance Song (b)

Recorded by BILLIE STEWART

(Catalog No. 2449)

A duplication of the preceding song was recorded by Billie Bowlegs, and a comparison of the two renditions is interesting. The opening phrase is the same but Bowlegs is not so proficient a singer as Stewart and the rendition is incomplete. This is an example of the manner in which a singer at a dance may be familiar with the opening of a song and join in it, while the leader is able to carry it through to a conclusion.

Duplication of No. 123.

(Catalog No. 2458)

Recorded by BILLIE BOWLEGS

BLACKBIRD DANCE

Four or five men and women perform this dance, which is only about 2 minutes in duration. The dancers imitate the actions of blackbirds, moving their arms like wings and "hopping up and down." The dance has only one song, which is sung by the man with the shell rattle. The dancers do not sing.

No. 124. Blackbird Dance Song

(Catalog No. 2446)

Recorded by BILLIE STEWART

Voice ♩ = 72
Rattle ♩ = 72
See **rhythm of rattle below.**

Rhythm of rattle ♩ ♩ ♩ ♩

BUZZARD DANCE

This is another dance in which the actions of a bird are imitated. Men, women, and boys take part in the dance and are "bunched together," not in any particular order. They extend their arms and raise one as they lower the other, after the manner of a large bird with outstretched wings, sailing rather than flying through the sky. Some dancers wear the feathers of a buzzard in their hair. Only one man sings, shaking a coconut shell rattle. Billie Stewart has been the leader of this, as of other dances. He recorded six songs of the dance but only two are presented, the others being variants of these melodies.

No. 125. Buzzard Dance Song (a)

(Catalog No. 2186)

Recorded by Billie Stewart

No. 126. Buzzard Dance Song (b)

(Catalog No. 2187)

Recorded by Billie Stewart

CATFISH DANCE

Among the imitative dances witnessed among the Menominee and Winnebago in Wisconsin was the Fish Dance, in which the action differed from the Catfish Dance of the Seminole. The Menominee dance was performed by men and women in a slightly stooping posture, with arms moving slowly, like fins. They squatted on the ground, continuing to move their arms with a finlike motion, and turned their heads to one side, they also moved forward dragging one leg at full length behind them (Densmore, 1932 a, p. 191). The Winnebago imitated the fish in the same manner.

A Seminole performance of the Catfish Dance was witnessed at a
Seminole wedding, presented at Coppinger's Tropical Gardens, an
exhibition village near Miami, on February 17, 1932. Panther sang
the songs, in which the dancers did not join. He was seated and shook
a coconut-shell rattle. Men and women take part in the dance, holding hands, and moving in couples around a circle. The women are
next the center of the circle. Each man moves his free arm below the
elbow in a sweeping manner, imitating the fin of a fish. Panther
said, "Sometimes they act as though they were going backwards."
The women wore knee rattles, as in the Gorn Dance and some others.
The rattles made no sound when the women were walking to join the
dance, but made a jingling sound when the women were dancing

No. 127. Catfish Dance Song (a)

(Catalog No. 2127)

Recorded by PANTHER

No. 128. Catfish Dance Song (b)

(Catalog No. 2128)

Recorded by PANTHER

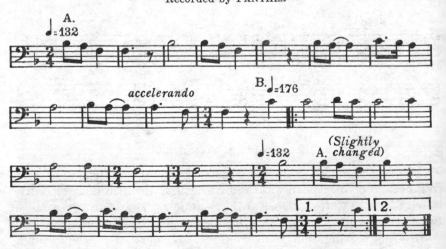

No. 129. Catfish Dance Song (c)

(Catalog No. 2129)

Recorded by PANTHER

Fine

No. 130. Catfish Dance Song (d)

(Catalog No. 2130)

Recorded by PANTHER

No. 131. Catfish Dance Song (e)

(Catalog No. 2464)

Recorded by BILLIE BOWLEGS

Voice ♩ = 116
Rattle ♩ = 116
See rhythm of rattle below.

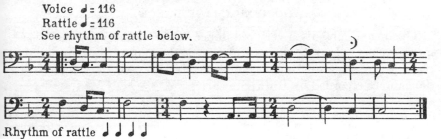

Rhythm of rattle ♩ ♩ ♩ ♩

TURKEY DANCE

Panther states that the people of the Turkey clan had this dance long ago and that only members of the clan took part in the dance at first. He said the members of this clan went to Oklahoma.

In this dance the singer sits at the east of the fire, holding a coconut-shell rattle which he shakes up and down. The men and women who take part in the dance are equal in number. The men form in a curved line on one side of the fire and the women in a similar line on the other side of the fire, all facing toward the east. Both lines advance, and when the leading man and woman meet, she puts the palms of her hands on the palms of his and places her left foot on top of his right foot and her right foot on top of his left foot. Thus he carries the entire weight of her body. In this position they dance a half circle, bringing each to the opposite side of the groups of dancers. Then she goes back of the line of men and he goes back of the women. Each couple does the same, and when all have gone through this motion the men are again on one side and the women on the other side. Then they repeat the action, or dance figure.

No. 132. Turkey Dance Song

(Catalog No. 2106)

Recorded by PANTHER

WHOOPING CRANE DANCE

This is undoubtedly a very old dance as the whooping crane [15] is almost extinct. In this dance the men and women move in couples, preceded by a man with a coconut-shell rattle. All the songs of this dance were recorded by Billie Stewart.

---

[15] "Whooping Crane, *Grus americana* (Linnaeus). Distribution : North America ; bred formerly from northern Mackenzie south to Illinois and Iowa ; now mainly restricted to southern Mackenzie and northern Saskatchewan ; in migration formerly not rare on the Atlantic coast from New England to Florida and casual west to Colorado and Idaho ; winters from the Gulf States to central Mexico." "The Whooping Crane is the only bird of North America that can be described as 'almost as tall as a man.'" "The virtual extermination, or at best the extreme rarity, of the great Whooping Crane, leaves the much smaller Sandhill Crane by far the largest representative of that interesting family in America." (Pearson, 1936, pt. 1, pp. 198, 200.)

No. 133. Whooping Crane Dance Song (a)

(Catalog No. 2425)

No. 134. Whooping Crane Dance Song (b)

(Catalog No. 2426)

Fine

No. 135. Whooping Crane Dance Song (c)

(Catalog No. 2427)

No. 136. Whooping Crane Dance Song (d)

(Catalog No. 2428)

SANDHILL CRANE DANCE

In the Sandhill Crane Dance the girls move in a circle in one direction and the men, also in a circle, move in the opposite direction. It was not ascertained which are in the inner circle. Five songs of this dance were recorded, but only four were transcribed.

No. 137. Sandhill Crane Dance Song (a)

(Catalog No. 2145)

Recorded by PANTHER

No. 138. Sandhill Crane Dance Song (b)

(Catalog No. 2146)

Recorded by PANTHER

No. 139. Sandhill Crane Dance Song (c)

(Catalog No. 2147)

Recorded by PANTHER

No. 140. Sandhill Crane Dance Song (d)

(Catalog No. 2148)

Recorded by PANTHER

SCREECH OWL DANCE

It was said this dance and its songs originated in the Cypress Swamp group and "did not belong to the people who went to Oklahoma." Both men and women take part in the dance, but only the men sing the songs. This is similar to the custom in the Snake Dance. The dancers are in a long line, alternating men and women, and moving in a circle, contraclockwise, around the fire. The leader of the line has a coconut-shell rattle in his right hand and extends his left arm backward, holding the right hand of the woman behind him. This is continued throughout the line. During the first and second songs the dancers stand still and during the third and fourth songs they move forward. This is the usage of the Cypress Swamp Seminole. Panther said the dance among the Cow Creek Seminole is slightly different, but members of one group often join in the dance of the other group. The melody of the second song was the same as that of the first and is not presented.

No. 141. Screech Owl Dance Song (a)

(Catalog No. 2107)

Recorded by PANTHER

No. 142. Screech Owl Dance Song (b)

(Catalog No. 2108)

Recorded by PANTHER

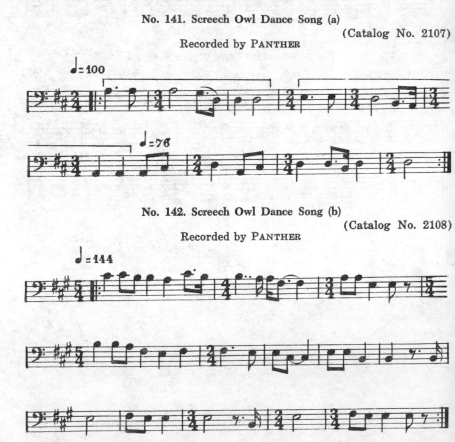

No. 143. Screech Owl Dance Song (c)
Recorded by PANTHER

(Catalog No. 2109)

This was advertised as a "prairie dance" when presented at a fair on the west coast of Florida. Panther designated this as an "off-hand name" for which there was no reason except that "white people understand that word 'prairie.'"

Billie Stewart, who recorded a song of this dance in the Cow Creek group, said "this song is one in five pieces." There was no pause between the parts of the song, but they were discernible. The entire performance was 2 minutes in length, only the third and fifth parts of the song being transcribed. The others were variants, with slight differences in note values or unimportant progressions. Between the renditions are the "inhaling" which occurs occasionally in Seminole songs.

No. 144. Screech Owl Dance Song (d)
Recorded by BILLIE STEWART

(Catalog No. 2448)

Section 3

Fine.

No. 144. Screech Owl Dance Song (d)—Continued

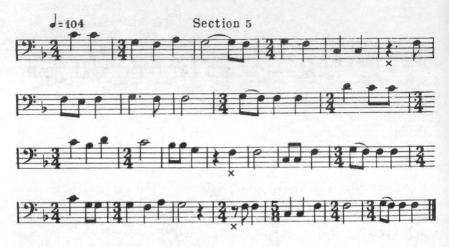

RABBIT DANCE

Men and women alternate in this dance, holding hands and moving around the man with the rattle for about 25 minutes. There is only one song for the dance and, according to Seminole custom, the dancers do not sing.

No. 145. Rabbit Dance Song

Recorded by BILLIE STEWART

(Catalog No. 2447

FOX DANCE

Men and women, boys and girls, take part in this dance. Following a leader they move around the fire in a zigzag path, in a counterclockwise direction. As in other dances, the singer is stationed east of the fire with his coconut-shell rattle, and the dancers do not sing. One song is sung with each encircling of the fire. When the leader returns to the east, the dancers stop for a few moments, then the singer begins another song and the dancers move again around the fire.

Eight songs of this dance were recorded but only five are presented. The untranscribed melodies were duplicates, probably having different words. All were recorded by Billie Stewart.

No. 146. Fox Dance Song (a)

(Catalog No. 2385)

No. 147. Fox Dance Song (b)

(Catalog No. 2386)

No. 148. Fox Dance Song (c)

(Catalog No. 2387)

No. 149. Fox Dance Song (d)

(Catalog No. 2388)

No. 150. Fox Dance Song (e)

(Catalog No. 2389)

SWITCHGRASS DANCE

The informant on this dance was Panther who said there is a tradition among the Seminole that a long time ago someone captured these Indians and sold them to white people. He did not know who captured the Indians or where it occurred, but said the songs of the Switchgrass Dance go back to that time. The dancers are men and women in alternate couples, two men leading the line, followed by two women, and so on to the end of the company. The singer, with his coconut-shell rattle, is in his usual position east of the fire. The six following songs of this dance in the Cypress Swamp group were recorded by Panther.

No. 151. Switchgrass Dance Song (a)

(Catalog No. 2132)

No. 152. Switchgrass Dance Song (b)

(Catalog No. 2133)

No. 153. Switchgrass Dance Song (c)

(Catalog No. 2134)

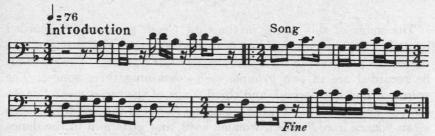

No. 154. Switchgrass Dance Song (d)

(Catalog No. 2135)

No. 155. Switchgrass Dance Song (e)

(Catalog No. 2136)

No. 156. Switchgrass Dance Song (f)

(Catalog No. 2137)

The songs of this dance in the Cow Creek group were recorded by Billie Stewart who said it is danced at night and that the men sometimes put grass in their turbans, like tall feathers. The six songs he recorded are in two groups, each containing three songs. The words of the first, second, and third songs of the series mean "dance easy." Then there is "talking," and the words of the last three songs mean "dance hard." Men, women, boys, and girls join in the dance around the fire but do not hold hands. The singer with his rattle is in the usual position at the east.

No. 157. Switchgrass Dance Song (g)

(Catalog No. 2311)

No. 158. Switchgrass Dance Song (h)

(Catalog No. 2312)

No. 159. Switchgrass Dance Song (i)

(Catalog No. 2313)

No. 160. Switchgrass Dance Song (j)

(Catalog No. 2314)

No. 161. Switchgrass Dance Song (k)

(Catalog No. 2315)

No. 162. Switchgrass Dance Song (l)

(Catalog No. 2316)

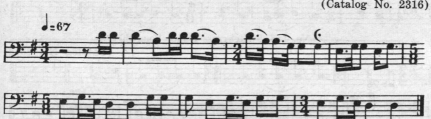

HAIR DANCE

The name of this dance is an example of the difficulty experienced in work without a competent interpreter. Billie Stewart called it the Bareheaded Dance. About two weeks later, Panther was consulted concerning the name and he said the correct name is tiwa'co (hair) pun'ka (dance) and that neither name has any significance, as the men wore their turbans while dancing. It is probable that the original meaning of the designation is lost, though the dance and its songs remain.

This dance was described by Panther who said that men and women take part and that the fire is in the middle of the dance circle, and that the opening of the circle is toward the west instead of toward the east, as in other dances. The singer, with his coconut-shell rattle, is between the fire and this opening. Men and women take part in the dance. At first, a man stands at each side of the opening of the dance circle. These two men step forward, shake hands and change places so that the man who stood at one side takes his place at the other side of the entrance. Then each goes to the spectators and invites a girl, bringing her to a place next him. Then she goes and brings a man who, in turn goes and brings a girl until the line on each side of the fire consists of men and girls in alternate order. When all are in position, the two leaders, side by side, move toward the south followed by the two girls (one from each side) who, in turn are followed by two men. Thus the pairs of men and girls alternate in a long dancing line. A song is sung as they circle the fire once, then they stop until the singer begins another song. All the songs of this dance were recorded by Billie Stewart.

No. 163. Hair Dance Song (a)

(Catalog No. 2390)

No. 164. Hair Dance Song (b)

(Catalog No. 2391)

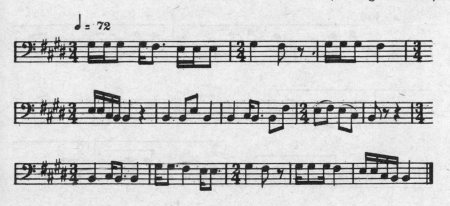

No. 165. Hair Dance Song (c)

(Catalog No. 2392)

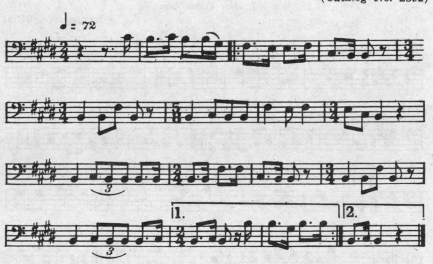

No. 166. Hair Dance Song (d)

(Catalog No. 2432)

No. 167. Hair Dance Song (e)

(Catalog No. 2433)

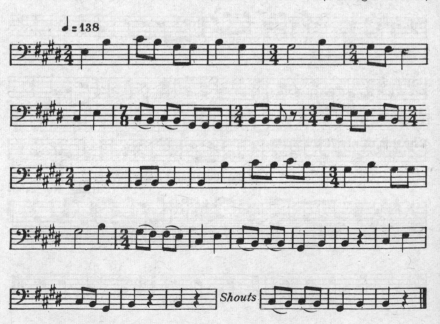

No. 168. Hair Dance Song (f)

(Catalog No. 2434)

♩ = 138

Fine

TWO-DIRECTION DANCE

The name of this dance was first translated "two-headed," and when questioned, the informant said the Seminole word meant "Headed in two directions." Both men and women take part in the dance and are in pairs, two men alternating with two women. These pairs of dancers, one behind another, move around the man with the coconut-shell rattle who is the only singer. They progress around him until they reach their starting-point, then they "stand still a minute" before reversing and moving in the opposite direction, singing a different song. When they have completed the circle again they reverse and repeat the performance with another song. Four songs were recorded, the second being a duplicate of the first, probably with different words.

No. 169. Two-direction Dance Song (a)

(Catalog No. 2435)

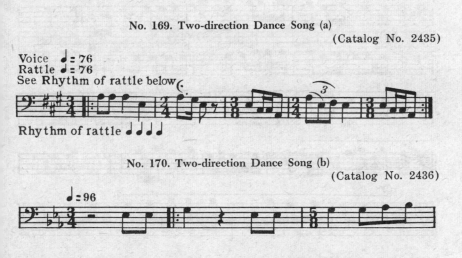

Voice ♩ = 76
Rattle ♩ = 76
See **Rhythm of rattle** below

Rhythm of rattle ♩ ♩ ♩ ♩

No. 170. Two-direction Dance Song (b)

(Catalog No. 2436)

♩ = 96

Fine

No. 171. Two-direction Dance Song (c)

(Catalog No. 2437)

STEAL-PARTNER DANCE

Concerning this dance it was said, "A man asks a girl and a girl asks a man to dance. A girl may be at one side. A boy can steal her and she will dance with him. After the dance she goes back." This information, though scanty, suggests a line in which boys and girls alternate, moving around the fire. The singer, with his rattle, is in the usual position between the fire and the entrance of the dance circle, toward the east.

No. 172. Steal Partner Dance Song (a)

(Catalog No. 2305)

Recorded by BILLIE STEWART

Fine

No. 173. Steal Partner Dance Song (b)

(Catalog No. 2306)

Recorded by BILLIE STEWART

Fine

No. 174. Steal Partner Dance Song (c)

(Catalog No. 2307)

Recorded by BILLIE STEWART

No, 175. Steal Partner Dance Song (d)

(Catalog No. 2308)

Recorded by BILLIE STEWART

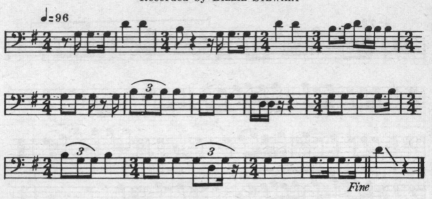

Fine

No. 176. Steal Partner Dance Song (e)

(Catalog No. 2309)

Recorded by BILLIE STEWART

No. 177. Steal Partner Dance Song (f)

Recorded by BILLIE STEWART

(Catalog No. 2310)

OLD DANCE

A certain old Seminole dance had only six songs, all of which were recorded. The name of the dance has been forgotten, but it is said that it could be danced at any time and that everyone took part in it. The dancers moved forward in pairs, two men, then two women, then two men, and so on. The motion, as in other Seminole dances, was counterclockwise. Billie Stewart was the singer for this dance and was stationed at the east of the fire, accompanying the songs with a coconut-shell rattle. The dancers did not sing.

No. 178. Song of an Old Dance (a)

Recorded by BILLIE STEWART

(Catalog No. 2076)

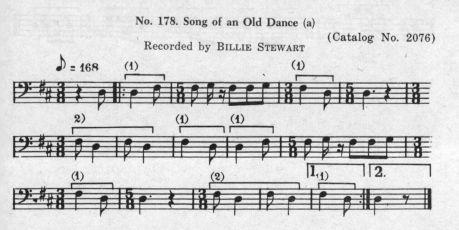

No. 179. Song of an Old Dance (b)

(Catalog No. 2077)

Recorded by BILLIE STEWART

No. 180. Song of an Old Dance (c)

(Catalog No. 2078)

Recorded by BILLIE STEWART

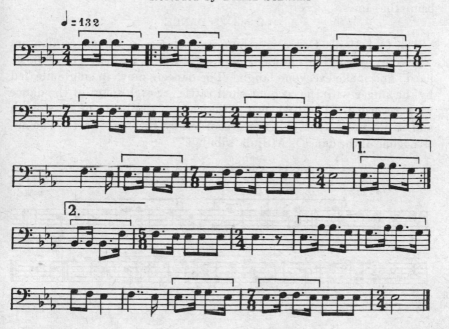

No. 181. Song of an Old Dance (d)

(Catalog No. 2079)

Recorded by BILLIE STEWART

Fine

The fifth song was the same melody as the fourth, and the final song differed from these two in having an introduction, the melody being the same.

OLD MAN'S DANCE

The Old Man's Dance is a humorous dance in which the dancers "dress up to look like old men," and each carries a cane. They "dance hard" and make everyone laugh. The dancers move in single file, led by the singer with the coconut-shell rattle. Seven songs of the dance were recorded. The fifth was practically a duplicate of the fourth and is not presented. All were recorded by Billie Stewart. The native name of the dance is A′djula′kibungë′.

No. 182. Old Man's Dance Song (a)

No. 183. Old Man's Dance Song (b)

No. 184. Old Man's Dance Song (c)

No. 185. Old Man's Dance Song (d)

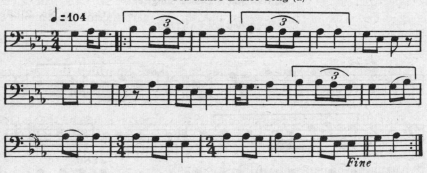

No. 186. Old Man's Dance Song (e)

No. 187. Old Man's Dance Song (f)

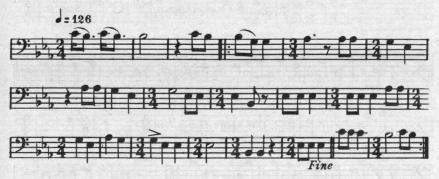

SNAKE DANCE

The Snake Dance is also called the Horned Owl, and is given in the evening, during the Hunting Dance. Men and women join in the dance, but the women do not sing. The motion of the line of dancers is around four corner posts, encircled one after another.

No. 188. Snake Dance Song (a)

Recorded by PANTHER

(Catalog No. 2125)

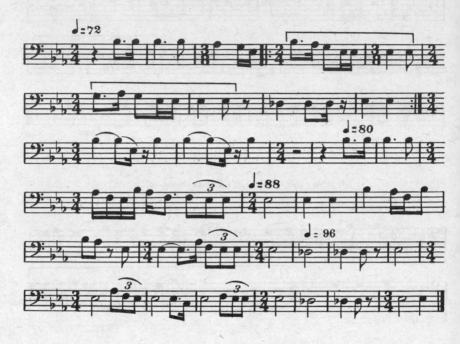

No. 189. Snake Dance Song (b)

Recorded by PANTHER

(Catalog No. 2126)

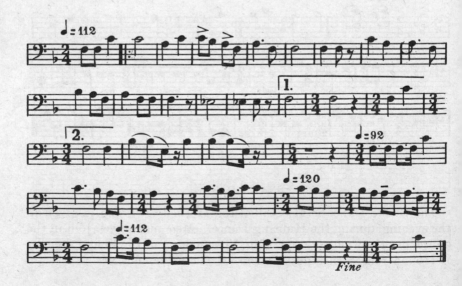

CRAWFISH DANCE

The Crawfish Dance and the dance next following are known as summer dances. Five songs of this dance were recorded by Billie Stewart, only three being transcribed. The others were duplicates or differed only in unimportant progressions. Men and girls join in the dance, alternating in the line, and holding hands. The songs are accompanied by a coconut-shell rattle.

No. 190. Crawfish Dance Song (a)

(Catalog No. 2429)

No. 191. Crawfish Dance Song (b)

(Catalog No. 2430)

No. 191. Crawfish Dance Song (b)—Continued

No. 192. Crawfish Dance Song (c)

(Catalog No. 2431)

DRUNKEN DANCE

Men and women take part in the Drunken Dance, which is also called the Crazy Dance. Informants said that intoxication was not connected with the dance but that the people acted without restraint, behaving like drunken men. William King, the Creek interpreter, said the Seminole term for the dance is honi'tĭc, meaning "wild, in the sense of untaught native or undisciplined," and that the Creek term is obung'kaha'tco. He said "It is the same as though children or anybody was happy and capered around."

This dance was studied by Dr. Frank G. Speck (1911, vol. 1, No. 2, pp. 190–200, 204–206) among the Creek and Yuchi Indians in Oklahoma, in 1904–1905, and several of its songs were recorded. He says, "One of the favorite Creek dances is the Crazy Dance, so named because the participants behave like wild people. The songs for the Crazy Dance usually are funny or obscene stories." Concerning the Drunken Dance he says, "The dancers reel, jostle one another, and act in general like drunken men." A parallel with early Greek culture is noted in the words of song No. 204. It seems possible this dance may be a survival of descriptions of Bacchanalian dances, given to the Seminole by Greek colonists (cf p. 171).

No. 193. Drunken Dance Song (a)

(Catalog No. 2444)

Recorded by Billie Stewart

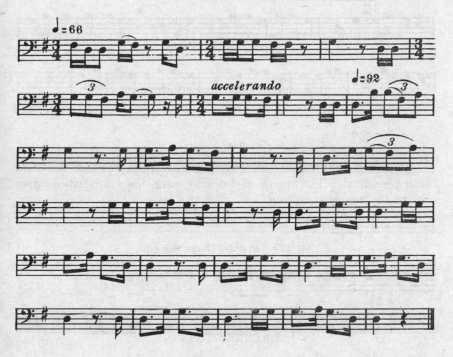

No. 194. Drunken Dance Song (b)

(Catalog No. 2445)

Recorded by Billie Stewart

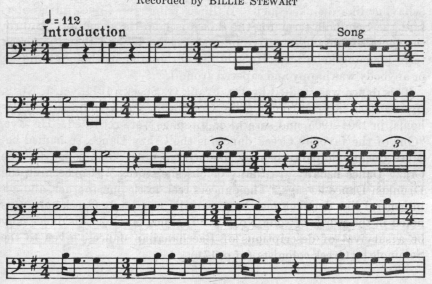

No. 194. Drunken Dance Song (b)—Continued

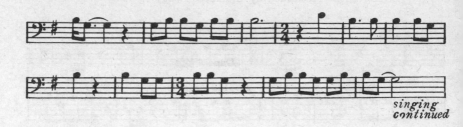

Three songs of this dance were recorded by Billie Bowlegs, only two being presented. The words of his first song, not transcribed, were said to be "about drinking."

No. 195. Drunken Dance Song (c)

(Catalog No. 2456)

Recorded by BILLIE BOWLEGS

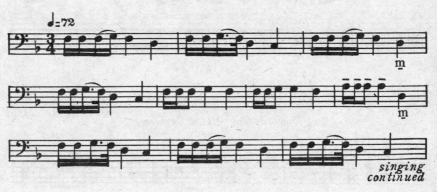

No. 196. Drunken Dance Song (d)

(Catalog No. 2457)

Recorded by BILLIE BOWLEGS

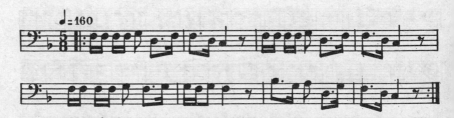

SKUNK DANCE

The Skunk Dance was a winter dance, and no information was obtained concerning it.

No. 197. Skunk Dance Song (a)

Recorded by BILLIE STEWART

(Catalog No. 2438)

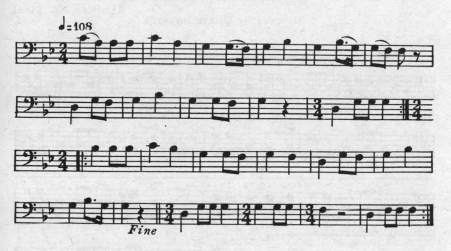

Fine

No. 198. Skunk Dance Song (b)

Recorded by BILLIE STEWART

(Catalog No. 2439)

CHILDREN'S DANCES

The little children are encouraged to dance in all Indian tribes. As soon as possible, they join in dances of the older people, and among the Seminole they had dances of their own.

No. 199. Lightningbug Dance Song

(Catalog No. 2459)

Recorded by BILLIE BOWLEGS

No. 200. "Little Bug" Dance Song

(Catalog No. 2460)

Recorded by BILLIE BOWLEGS

Translation.—The bug bites.

In the next dance the children imitated a little fish (drĭm). This
was said to be a favorite dance (cf. imitative dances p. 104).

No. 201. "Little Fish" Dance

Recorded by BILLIE BOWLEGS

(Catalog No. 2461)

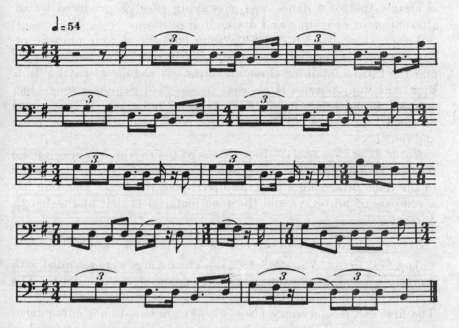

Three songs of the next dance were recorded, but only one could
be transcribed. The action was not described.

No. 202. Little Boys' Dance

Recorded by BILLIE BOWLEGS

(Catalog No. 2463)

ANALYSES OF SOCIAL AND CHILDREN'S DANCE SONGS

ALLIGATOR DANCE SONGS—CYPRESS SWAMP GROUP

No. 64 (Cat. No. 2122).—Three consecutive renditions of this song were recorded and show no differences. The song opens with a major tetrachord on G, followed by a major third. This is followed by a minor tetrachord on E followed by the same major third. The rhythm is clearly that of a dance, and a swaying effect is produced by an alternation of ascending and descending phrases.

No. 65 (Cat. No. 2123).—This song consists of four phrases, or melodic periods, the first, second, and fourth containing two measures and the third containing three measures. A change of rhythm in a song with four phrases is unusual in recorded Seminole songs, but occurs frequently in songs of the southern Plains, especially in songs of the Ghost Dance. The tone material is that of a major triad and fourth.

No. 66 (Cat. No. 2124).—Repetitions of the rhythmic unit comprise this entire melody. Two renditions were recorded without a break in the time, producing a long, uninterrupted rhythm. The song has a compass of an octave and the tone material is that of the fourth 5-toned scale.

ALLIGATOR DANCE SONGS—COW CREEK GROUP

Nos. 67–73 (Cat. Nos. 2298–2304).—These songs were recorded with scarcely a break in the time and will be considered as a unit. The pitch is the same in all the songs, but there is variety in the rhythm. The first and second songs (Nos. 67, 68) are based on a minor triad and minor seventh, the tones being in descending order, as usual in this material. The third and fourth songs (Nos. 69, 70) are based on the tones of a minor triad and the fifth song (No. 71) is based on a major triad. The sixth song (No. 72) contains only two tones, a whole tone apart. Although the tone material is scanty, this melody has a definite and interesting rhythm. The final song of the series (No. 73) is based on triads and thirds, and was followed by the glissando phrases that follow Seminole dance songs. The series as a whole is characterized by triads and thirds in the framework of the melodies. Other series with what may be termed group individuality are the Switchgrass Dance songs of the Cow Creek group which are based on fourths and tetrachords (cf. p. 164) and the songs of the Whooping Crane Dance which are major in tonality and have other characteristics in common (cf. p. 161).

BABY ALLIGATOR DANCE SONGS

Nos. 74, 75 (Cat. Nos. 2442, 2443).—The framework of both these songs consists of overlapping triads, each continuing for at least five measures. This produces an alternation of major and minor phrases,

the tones of the two triads occurring in descending order in the sixth
and seventh measures of both songs. After the pause and change of
tempo the order of the triads is reversed, the minor triad preceding
the major. This resembles the final phrase of No. 77 so closely as to
suggest a possibility that the two pairs of songs may belong to the
same dance, the native name being differently translated. This pair
of songs was recorded in 1932 and the other in 1933. Both were followed by shouts instead of the usual glissando phrases.

LIZARD DANCE SONGS

Nos. 76, 77 (Cat. Nos. 2440, 2441).—Except for the descent to D
and C, these melodies are based on the tonic triad. They are particularly good examples of the swaying motion frequently noted in Seminole dance songs. They resemble one another so closely as to suggest they may be two versions of the same song. They were followed
by shouts similar to those that followed the songs of the preceding
dance.

BIRD DANCE SONGS—CYPRESS SWAMP GROUP

Nos. 78–91 (Cat. Nos. 2092–2105).—A rise in pitch and period formation occur in Nos. 78, 81, and 85 of this series. As in other Seminole songs with this form, the rise in pitch is more gradual than in
Pueblo songs, but the higher pitch is established at the opening of
Period B. In No. 78 the pitch is a semitone higher at this point, the
gradual rise continued and the second rendition was begun a whole
tone higher than the first, this pitch being maintained to the end of
the performance. The melodic structure and tone material of Nos.
79 and 80 is the same, but the rhythm is entirely different. The sixteenth notes at the close of the first and similar measures in No. 80
were little more than pulsations of the voice. In songs with period
formation the second period is generally more lively than the first,
but in No. 81 the rhythm of this period is more even and steady than
that of the first. It is followed by a repetition of the first period
with slight changes. The general form of No. 82 is different from
that of the preceding songs in the group. The melody lies almost
entirely above the keynote and contains no rhythmic unit, though
several measures begin with the same count division which occurs in
both double and triple measures. Two half notes give steadiness
to the rhythm of the song as a whole. No. 83 appears to be a duplication of No. 29, recorded by Charlie Billie. The present song was
recorded by Panther who expressed concern lest Charlie Billie may
have recorded songs of incidental dances that were mistaken for ceremonial songs of the Corn Dance. Such an error was possible, as
Charlie Billie spoke no English and his songs were recorded without
a competent interpreter and under difficult conditions. Panther did
not hear Charlie Billie's recordings and a duplication could only have

been detected after the songs were transcribed. A comparison of the two transcriptions suggests such a duplication. A major third is prominent in Charlie Billie's rendition and a minor triad and seventh were clearly sung by Panther, but Charlie Billie's intonation was somewhat uncertain while Panther sang all his song with confidence. Almost every phrase in No. 84 is descending in trend and the rhythmic unit shows an interesting variation in the fifth and sixth measures. Several renditions were recorded. No. 85 resembles a dancing song of the Cocopa Indians in its rhythmic repetitions of the upper tones of a major triad (cf. Densmore, 1932 b, No. 115). Periods A and B alternate, the former being slightly changed in its recurrence, giving variety to the rhythm. Another variation is produced by the change of accent in the rhythmic units, the first ending on an accented and the second on an unaccented part of the measure. The compass is limited to a major triad except for the descent of a fourth, near the close of certain phrases. Descending phrases are prominent in the framework of Nos. 86 and 87, and the change of tempo in the latter was given in all the renditions. A strange resemblance exists between No. 88 and a Chippewa song. The first measures of this song are the same as in a Chippewa love song recorded in northern Minnesota in 1907 except that in the Chippewa song two quarter notes occur instead of a half note in the first and fourth measures. The general pattern of the melody is the same (cf. Densmore, 1910, No. 138). Three flats occur in the melody which is transcribed as it was sung but the sequence of tones does not suggest E-flat as the keynote. Two tetrachords are prominent in the melody, generally occurring in descending progression. Two descending fourths form the framework of No. 89, comprising the compass of an octave. This bears some resemblance to the song next preceding in its use of a descending fourth followed by a descent of a whole tone. Four phrases constitute No. 90, the rhythmic unit occurring in all except the final phrase. The measure next the final measure contains, in its third count, the same count divisions as the last count in the rhythmic unit, followed by a phrase like the fourth measure. This thematic treatment is particularly interesting. After singing the song as transcribed the singer repeated the performance without a break in the time. The first five measures of No. 91 suggest a major tonality, but the final measures emphasize the tone D and the song ends on a minor third. The final measure carries the rhythm forward to a repetition of the song.

The songs of this dance are in sets of four, and after each set the dancers stand in their places and pause. It is uncertain whether entire sets of songs are presented in the foregoing series.

CHICKEN DANCE SONGS

No. 92 (Cat. No. 2188).—The rendition of this song was a semitone higher than the transcription. The melody is based on a major triad, though the minor third below the keynote is a prominent tone. The tone material is that of the fourth 5-toned scale. The measures in 5–8 time control the rhythm of the song as a whole and give it stability.

No. 93 (Cat. No. 2189).—This melody is based on the second 5-toned scale and the rhythm is entirely different from that of the preceding song. It is slower in tempo and contains smaller count divisions. The rhythmic unit occurs in both double and triple measures, the additional tone in the latter giving variety to the rhythm.

No. 94 (Cat. No. 2190).—This song contains 12 measures and 25 progressions, which is an unusual freedom of movement. The compass of six tones and the melody touches the highest and lowest tones of the compass in the second measure. No rhythmic unit occurs, though the song is rhythmic in character and contains the swaying motion of the dance. This song was recorded on two cylinders, the second containing three renditions. The first phrase was the same in all renditions, also the measure in 5–8 time. The only differences consist in the number of repetitions of the keynote and other unimportant features of the melody.

No. 95 (Cat. No. 2191).—The keynote is the lowest tone in this song and the melody is based on the tonic triad. The sixth above the keynote is prominent but does not occur as an accented tone. The general trend of the melody is downward, the descending intervals being about three times as many as the ascending intervals. The repeated portion was sung several times.

BLACK GRASS DANCE SONGS

No. 96 (Cat. No. 2422).—This and the two following songs of the same dance are characterized by clear, rhythmic structure. This song consists of three phrases, each containing two measures. A rhythmic unit occurs in the first and last phrases, and the fourth measure contains the same count divisions as the rhythmic unit but differently accented. The principal interval is a descending fourth and the song is minor in tonality.

No. 97 (Cat. No. 2423).—In contrast to the preceding song, this melody progresses chiefly by major and minor thirds. The opening phrase is based on a major triad, followed by a phrase on a minor triad and a recurrence of the measures in 3–8 and 2–4 time. The singing of this was followed by a repetition of No. 96 with slight changes in unimportant note values.

No. 98 (Cat. No. 2424).—Descending phrases of a fourth characterize this song. In the opening measures these occur as D–A and G–D, descending an octave in the second measure. In next to the final measure the descending interval G–D is repeated. The song consists of two phrases and the rhythmic form is simple and unusually interesting. The tone material is that of the fourth 5-toned scale.

STOMP DANCE SONGS

Nos. 99–104 (Cat. Nos. 2393–2398).—There is an interesting uniformity in the six songs of this series. All are major in tonality and are characterized by a dotted eighth note, generally occurring on the accented count of the measure. Five of the songs contain a rhythmic unit (Nos. 99, 100, 101, 103, 104) and all except Nos. 102 and 103 begin with an ascending progression. A majority of the songs have the small compass of 3 to 6 tones, one (No. 103) has a compass of an octave and one (No. 101) has a range of 11 tones which is unusually large in Seminole songs. The melodies are framed chiefly on thirds and triads. With these resemblances it is interesting to note that no two songs are in the same tempo. Attention is directed to No. 101 in which the measure rhythms of the rhythmic unit are reversed in the two measures that follow the pause. The fifth and sixth measures in this section also contain an interesting variant of the rhythmic unit.

HINATA DANCE SONGS

Nos. 105–121 (Cat. Nos. 2399–2415).—This group of 17 songs contains interesting contrasts to the group next preceding, both groups being recorded by Billie Stewart. The compass in this group is larger. Only one song (No. 117) has a compass of less than an octave, and two (Nos. 111, 114) have a compass of 10 tones. The prevailing tempo is slow, 12 songs having a tempo of ♩=76 or less. The same number begin with a downward progression. Ten of the songs contain no rhythmic unit, which is an unusually large proportion of such melodies. Tetrachords and intervals of a fourth are more prominent than in the preceding group, though such songs may contain or end with a descending triad, as in Nos. 112, 113, and 114. One song (No. 110) progresses entirely by major and minor thirds. With these differences, it is interesting to note that these resemble the preceding songs in tonality, all except Nos. 106 and 118 being major in tonality.

QUAIL DANCE SONGS

No. 122 (Cat. No. 2131).—The Quail Dance is the first of several dances in which the actions of birds and animals are imitated (cf. p. 104). The first part of this song is sung as the dancers pretend to pick

up food like a quail, and the second part is sung as they dance. The
short opening phrase is the same in the two parts but in the second
it is extended into a dance rhythm. This song offers an interesting
study in rhythm which is too detailed for present consideration.

No. 123 (Cat. No. 2449).—This song and its repetition (Cat. No.
2458) were recorded by members of the Cow Creek group. The preceding song of the same dance was recorded by a member of the Cypress Swamp group. The song is evidently the same in the two versions but the first rendition, by Billie Stewart, contains measures in
7–8 time while the second rendition, by Billie Bowlegs, is in a simple
rhythm. It will be recalled that Billie Stewart is a leader in the
dances and considered an expert singer, while Billie Bowlegs "knows
some of the old songs." This is an important example of the simplifi-
cation of an old melody by a less qualified singer. Such tests have
been made in other tribes, with the same result. Several repetitions
of No. 123 were recorded and in some instances the second tone in
the first and second measures was sung as A instead of G, thus dupli-
cating the intervals in the opening measures of the second version of
the song. It will be noted that the first version is major and the second
is minor in tonality. This change in tonality is effected by the interval
of a fourth instead of a major third at the opening of the third
measure.

BLACKBIRD DANCE SONG

No. 124 (Cat. No. 2446).—In this dance the men and women imitate the motion of the blackbird's wings and "hop up and down." A
fluttering rhythm and decided accents characterize the song, with an
accelerated tempo which is maintained to the close of the performance. The increase in tempo is slight, but definite. The melody
progresses chiefly by major and minor thirds.

BUZZARD DANCE SONGS

No. 125 (Cat. No. 2186).—This melody was repeated many times
with no differences except that in one rendition a triplet of eighth notes
was substituted for the indicated count division on the opening count
of one measure. The tempo is slow and the alternation of ascending
and descending intervals suggests the graceful motion of the dancers.
The melody consists of four phrases, two followed by rests and two ending in measures in 3–8 time which carry the rhythm forward to the
next phrase.

No. 126 (Cat. No. 2187).—The rhythm of this melody is less simple
than that of the preceding song. The alternation of descending and
ascending intervals in the third and fourth measures is interesting,
and the song is classified as irregular in tonality.

CATFISH DANCE SONGS

No. 127 (Cat. No. 2127).—Three tetrachords form the framework of this melody, and the song closes with a repetition of a fourth (C–F) in a lower register. The song is major in tonality and a whole tone constitutes more than half the number of intervals. Variety is given to the rhythm by three measures in double time, occurring midway the length of the song.

No. 128 (Cat. No. 2128).—This melody is typical of the songs in period formation, the second period being higher, shorter, and more lively than the first and followed by a return of the first period, with slight changes. A descending tetrachord forms the framework of the first period, followed by a descending major triad. The second period is based on the same triad with the addition of the sixth on an unaccented count. Two renditions were recorded, being separated by a short pause. The renditions showed no differences.

No. 129 (Cat. No. 2129).—This is a lively melody with two simple rhythmic units. The first phrase is based on a descending tetrachord and the second phrase is based on minor third followed by three descending tetrachords (C–A–G, G–F–D, and F–D–C). The song closes with the descending tetrachord D–C–A and a return to C, the fifth above the keynote. The only progressions are minor thirds and whole tones, the song contains no change of measure lengths, and the compass is 11 tones. These three peculiarities are unusual in recorded Indian songs.

No. 130 (Cat. No. 2130).—This song, like the preceding, contains no change of measure lengths. It consists of an introductory measure and four phrases, the first, second, and fourth having the same rhythm The alternation of descending and ascending intervals produces the swaying motion that has been noted in many Seminole dance songs. Several renditions were recorded without a pause.

No. 131 (Cat. No. 2462).—This song was recorded by Billie Bowlegs, of the Cow Creek group, the preceding songs of this dance being recorded by Panther, of the Cypress Swamp group. It was sung a semitone higher than the transcription, with accompaniment of a rattle in quarter-note values coincident with the melody. Two descending tetrachords occur in the third and fourth measures, followed by two measures in triple time and a return of the tetrachord in double time. Except for one low tone, the compass of the melody is only five tones.

TURKEY DANCE SONG

No. 132 (Cat. No. 2106).—Two separate renditions of this song were recorded, the transcription being from the second. The same rhythm occurred in the first rendition, but there were unimportant differences in progressions. Three descending intervals of a fourth form the framework of the melody and appear consecutively in the first and second measures. The song has a compass of an octave. The lowest tone of the compass occurs twice during the melody which ends on the keynote, midway the compass. An additional count in the fifth measure gives character to the song as a whole. There is a suggestion of Scotch music in this song, and it is recalled that the Seminole were in contact with Scotch settlers at an early date.

WHOOPING CRANE DANCE SONGS

Nos. 133–136 (Cat. Nos. *2425–2428*).—All the songs of this group are major in tonality. The keynote of the first is E-flat and the keynote of the others is E. All the songs lie partly above and partly below the keynote and the compass varies from 6 to 11 tones. The tempo is about the same throughout the entire series. The rhythmic form of No. 133 is clear and interesting, with its repetition of the rhythmic unit on a lower tone. Two rhythmic units occur in No. 134 and the song as a whole has a distinct rhythmic form. Attention is directed to the fifth measure in which an eighth followed by two sixteenth notes occurs on the unaccented count of the measure. This has previously occurred on the accented count. Nos. 135 and 136 were sung without a break in the time. This pair of songs opens with four repeated tones, and the melody consists chiefly of whole tone progressions. The final song of the group (No. 136) opens with a measure in a high register, followed by two measures that resemble No. 134. A new rhythm is then introduced and the close of the melody has a compass of an octave.

SANDHILL CRANE DANCE SONGS

No. 137 (*Cat. No. 2145*).—The rhythm of this song as a whole is interesting, and its many repetitions by the dancers would constitute a larger unit. Attention is directed to the change from triple to double time in the third measure, with a return to triple time in the eighth measure, which contains the same count divisions as the first measure. Two descending tetrachords occur in the fifth and sixth measures. The pitch was gradually raised a semitone, the transcription being on the pitch of the opening measures. The new pitch level was maintained to the close of the performance.

No. 138 (*Cat. No. 2146*).—Overlapping tetrachords occur in the first and second measures of this song, and tetrachords occur frequently throughout the melody. Except in the opening measures, the song is in 3–8 time. A quarter or dotted eighth note occurs on the first count of each measure, and the one-measure phrases seem appropriate to this dance. The pitch was raised a semitone during the performance. The song next recorded was practically a duplicate of this melody and was not transcribed.

No. 139 (Cat. No. 2147).—The rather monotonous rhythm of this melody is occasionally varied by measures in 7–8 time. The melody is framed on the descending tetrachord F–E flat-C, with E-flat as the most frequent tone. It is a melody with much freedom and can scarcely be compared to songs with a keynote, though the tones are those of the fourth 5-toned scale. Several renditions were recorded.

No. 140 (Cat. No. 2148).—This song, like the preceding, is based on the descending tetrachord F–E flat-C, with an insistence upon E-flat which occurs five times as a half note. The song is classified as irregular in tonality. The phrases are short and each is followed by a rest. Attention is directed to the change to slower time near the close, with a return to the original tempo.

SCREECH OWL DANCE SONGS

No. 141 (Cat. No. 2107).—Three renditions of this song were recorded, separated by short pauses. Each rendition repeated the melody as presented except for an unimportant difference of progression on the final count of the sixth measure. The tones are those of the first 5-toned scale. The framework of the first and second phrases consists of two fifths, each enclosing a fourth. The song closes with a tetrachord followed by repeated minor thirds. The descending progressions are seven and the ascending progressions are six in number.

No. 142 (Cat. No. 2108).—Eight consecutive renditions of this song were recorded and are identical in every respect. The framework consists of a descending triad or fifth followed by an ascending interval and a descent of a fourth. This begins on C sharp and is re-repeated on B, followed by an additional descending fourth in the seventh measure. The remainder of the melody is characterized by fourths. The song is based on the fourth 5-toned scale and has a compass of nine tones.

No. 143 (Cat. No. 2109).—This song, like No. 141, is based on the first 5-toned scale. Two overlapping tetrachords comprise the rhythmic unit, and the song closes with a descent and ascent of a whole tone. The intervals comprise 10 descending and five ascending progressions.

No. 144 (Cat. No. 2448).—This song was recorded by Billie Stewart, of the Cow Creek group, the preceding songs of this dance being recorded by Panther, of the Cypress Swamp group. Stewart said "this is one song in five pieces." Probably each section was used with one circling around the fire in the dance. Only the third and fifth of these sections were transcribed. Each was interrupted by the forcible inhaling of breath that is a custom of the Seminole (cf. p. 215). The melody is based on successive tetrachords, a form frequently noted in this series. The compass is nine tones and the melody moves with freedom from its highest to its lowest tone.

RABBIT DANCE SONG

No. 145 (Cat. No. 2447).—A descent of nine tones occurs in the opening measures of this song and an ascending seventh occurs midway of its length. The melody is particularly active, and lacks the rhythmic coherence of many Seminole songs. The phrases are short and followed by rests. Attention is directed to the repeated tones between renditions and at the close of the song.

FOX DANCE SONGS

Nos. 146–150 (Cat. Nos. 2385–2389).—All the songs of this series have the same keynote and the count divisions consist chiefly of quarter and eighth notes. A majority begin in triple time. The characteristics of individual songs will be noted. Nos. 146 and 147 are in the same tempo and begin on the same tone. The interval of a fourth is prominent in both songs, and they resemble one another in the descending and ascending sequence of intervals that produce the swaying motion of Seminole dances. No. 148 is more rapid and the interval of a fourth is less prominent. The melody descends from the highest to the lowest tone of the compass in the first three measures, after which the trend of the melody is similar to that of the previous songs of the series. Another song was recorded but the melody was found to be similar to No. 148. Probably it contained different words, as the Indians consider a song to be different if the words are changed. In No. 149 the tempo is again increased and the minor third is the most prominent interval. The final song of the series (No. 150) is major in tonality but the most prominent interval is a minor third. The count divisions in the last measures of the opening phrase are reversed in succeeding measures, showing an interesting control of rhythm. The song has a compass of six tones, with the keynote as its highest tone.

SWITCHGRASS DANCE SONGS

Nos. 151–162 (Cat. Nos. 2132–2137, 2311–2316).—Six songs of this series were recorded by Panther of the Cypress Swamp group and six by Billie Stewart of the Cow Creek group. It is interesting to note that a majority of the songs in the series are in the same tempo ($\bullet$=76). As the two series differ in many other respects they will be considered separately.

Cypress Swamp group Nos. 151–156 (Cat. Nos. 2132–2137).—The first song of this series is based on two descending tetrachords, occurring consecutively in the second measure, followed by a minor triad. Attention is directed to a comparison between the last measure and a phrase consisting of the third measure and first count of the fourth measure. Such changes of accent are more apparent in several consecutive renditions than in a single rendition, as they give character to the performance as a whole. Five renditions of the second song (No. 152) were recorded and show no difference except an occasional shortening of the connective phrase. The melody is minor in tonality, beginning on the highest and ending on the lowest tone of the compass. The next song (No. 153) contains 22 progressions in six measures and is an unusually fluent melody. Tetrachords are prominent in the framework of the song which is minor in tonality and lacks the second tone of the complete octave. Four consecutive renditions of No. 154 were recorded and show no differences except that the connective measure was omitted between the third and fourth renditions. The melody is based on the fourth 5-toned scale and progresses chiefly by whole tones. Two rhythmic units occur in No. 155, one seeming to answer the other. The first unit begins on the highest tone of the compass and has a descending trend while the second unit contains the lowest tone of the compass and is on the same tones in both its occurrences. The tetrachord is prominent but the melody progresses chiefly by minor thirds. Three consecutive renditions were recorded. The two sections of No. 156 differ in tempo in each of the four renditions. An interesting contrast occurs in the closing progressions of the rhythmic unit, these being an ascending interval in the first and a descending interval in the second instance. The song is major in tonality and lacks the second and seventh tones of the complete octave.

Cow Creek group Nos. 157–162 (Cat. Nos. 2311–2316).—This series of songs is characterized by freedom of motion and consecutive descending fourths. These do not contain the swaying melodic motion and rhythm that characterize many Seminole dance songs. The tempo is the same throughout this series and the compass of each is an octave except No. 158, which has a range of only seven tones. The melody of No. 159 is based on intervals of a fourth. The signature indicates the pitch of the tones, not a keynote. An interesting resemblance occurs between the first and second rhythmic units in No. 160.

HAIR DANCE SONGS

Nos. 163–168 (Cat. Nos. 2390–2392, 2432–2434).—The first song of this group (No. 163) has a compass of an octave, beginning on the highest tone and descending to the lowest in three measures. It is formed on tetrachords and whole tones, and the rhythmic unit occurs in measures of three lengths. The second song (No. 164) is a particularly good dance song, with frequent alternation of ascending and descending intervals. The general form of the third song (No. 165) resembles that of No. 163 but contains smaller count divisions and has a more lively rhythm. The next song (No. 166) contains only eighth and quarter notes with two half notes, producing a smooth, simple rhythm. The compass is 11 tones, which is unusual in Seminole songs. A distinction was made between the eighth notes that are slurred together and those sung separately. A short rhythmic unit characterizes No. 167, occurring five times consecutively in the opening measures and appearing again at the close of the song. Like many other Seminole songs it is based on tetrachords, occurring in the upper and lower registers. The song has a compass of 11 tones and a steadily descending trend. The final song of the series (No. 168) has the same general form as the preceding songs of the same dance. Attention is directed to the consecutive tetrachords in the fifth and sixth measures. Two other songs of this dance were recorded but not transcribed, as they contained no characteristics not noted in the preceding songs.

TWO-DIRECTION DANCE SONGS

Nos. 169–171 (Cat. Nos. 2435–2437).—The songs of this dance are short and without rhythmic units. No. 169 is framed on descending tetrachords. Many repetitions were recorded, and were accompanied by the shaking of a rattle in quarter-note values, corresponding to the tempo of the song. Following this, another song was recorded but was not transcribed. In contrast to the preceding song, Nos. 170 and 171 are framed on triads, the former song being partly above and partly below the keynote, while the keynote is the lowest tone in the latter song. Ten repetitions of this song were recorded, the only difference being that the initial tone was sung as G instead of A in the last rendition.

STEAL-PARTNER DANCE SONGS

Nos. 172–177 (Cat. Nos. 2305–2310).—These songs were recorded in rapid succession and seemed to constitute a set. The keynote and general plan of all these songs is the same. They are based on a major triad with occasional passing tones. The second above the keynote is the passing tone in Nos. 172 and 173, the fourth in Nos. 174 and 177, and the sixth in No. 176, while No. 174 contains only the tones of the triad. All the songs except No. 174 have a compass of an octave, the melody lying partly above and partly below the keynote. All except Nos. 176 and 177 begin with an ascending progression. No. 173 is interesting but brief and it seems possible the introduction may be extended if desired. The sharp inhalation of breath, indicated by ✕, is described on p. 215.

SONGS OF AN OLD DANCE

No. 178 (Cat. No. 2176).—A change of accent gives variety to the rhythm of this song, the accent being transferred from a quarter to an eighth note in the second rhythmic unit. Only three tones occur in the melody, these being a fundamental and its major third and perfect fourth. The intervals are the same in both ascending and descending progression and comprise eight major thirds and four semitones.

No. 179 (Cat. No. 2177).—The regularity noted in the preceding song appears also in this melody, the ascending and descending intervals being equal in number. This is a fluent melody containing 24 measures and 48 progressions, 20 of which are minor thirds. The rhythm is distinctly that of a dance. The first seven measures were repeated at the close of the performance, which occurs in several other songs recorded by this singer.

No. 180 (Cat. No. 2178).—A rapid and lively dance song is here presented, with a simple framework consisting of a major triad with the second as an accented tone. The descent to the fifth below the keynote gives a graceful swing to the melody.

No. 181 (Cat. No. 2179).—This song was recorded on two cylinders, the first performance consisting of several renditions and the second consisting of only one rendition. The repetitions of the song were alike and the endings of the two performances were uniform. The song ends on the tone above its keynote. Exclusive of the closing phrase, the song consists of four periods, identical in rhythm except for the opening count of one measure.

An additional song of this dance was recorded but not transcribed, as the melody was a duplication of No. 181.

OLD MAN'S DANCE SONGS

Nos. 182–187 (Cat. Nos. 2416–2421).—All these songs are short, and have the same keynote, all begin on the first count of the measure, and all except one begin in double time. All the songs of this dance are based on a major triad and in all except Nos. 185 and 187 the entire melody lies above the keynote. In those songs there is a descent to the fifth below the keynote. Only two of the songs contain a rhythmic unit. The change to triple time in the seventh measure of No. 182 introduces a variant of the rhythmic unit. The measures in 3–8 time give variety to the rhythm of No. 183. Attention is directed to the slurred tones and tied notes in No. 184, also to the ascent of nine tones in three measures. A majority of the melody of No. 185 lies in its upper register, which is unusual in Indian songs. This is a graceful melody, with a smooth, even trend. An irregular rhythm is the chief interest in No. 186, and the series closes with No. 187, which is distinguished by a sharp accent at the beginning of a triple measure, near the end of the song.

SNAKE DANCE SONGS

Nos. 188, 189 (Cat. Nos. 2125, 2126).—This pair of songs has an interesting individuality. Both songs contain frequent changes of tempo and an unusual number of progressions, they also contain the sequence of ascending and descending whole tones that was noted in Nos. 141 and 143 recorded by the same singer. The second song is better adapted to dancing than the first and consists of two sections, separated by glissando tones. There is a resemblance to the period formation in both songs but this is not established.

CRAWFISH DANCE SONGS

Nos. 190–192 (Cat. Nos. 2429–2431).—Each of the opening phrases of No. 190 contains two measures, and one phrase seems to answer the other. Two-measure phrases continue throughout the melody which is based on a minor triad and sixth. The second song (No. 191) contains the same keynote and tone material except for one descent to B. Measures in quadruple time occur very rarely in Indian songs, but the measures transcribed in this time contain no secondary accent. The song closes with short phrases in slower time and a different rhythm. The third song (No. 192) is major in tonality and contains the tones of the fourth 5-toned scale. The change from a minor to its relative major "key" is interesting and unusual. As in other songs of this dance, the phrases consist of two measures and generally end with a descending progression.

DRUNKEN DANCE SONGS

Nos. 193–196 (Cat. Nos. 2444, 2445, 2446, 2457).—The first of these melodies (No. 193) is somewhat incoherent, containing many rests but few complete phrases. The relation of the tones to a keynote is not clear, although the prominence of G and D suggest the former as a keynote. The second song (No. 194) was preceded by exclamations. It contains frequent rests and an unusual number of half notes. The opening phrases are based on a minor third, after which the song contains only the tones of a major third. The count divisions are simple and consist chiefly of eighth notes. Nos. 195 and 196 were recorded by a different singer and the songs are different in character. They contain many small count divisions, are small in compass, and are scanty in melodic and rhythmic material. No. 195 was recorded with a rattle but the rhythm of the rattle is not clear.

SKUNK DANCE SONGS

Nos. 197, 198 (Cat. Nos. 2438, 2439).—The phrases in No. 197 consist chiefly of two measures and are in pairs, the second seeming to answer the first. The melody is minor in tonality, with an interesting prominence of a descent to the seventh followed by a return to the keynote. The count divisions are simple and the melody is small in compass. The next song (No. 198) is much slower in tempo and the phrases generally consist of single measures, including an eighth rest. The song is major in tonality and has a compass of an octave. The answering phrases resemble those in the first song of the dance.

CHILDREN'S DANCE SONGS

Nos. 199–202 (*Cat. Nos. 2459, 2460, 2461, 2463*).—Strong accents characterize No. 199 which contains no change of measure lengths until the final phrase. The compass is small, the tempo is unusually slow, and the rhythmic unit is long. The melody does not suggest the subject of the dance. No. 200 was recorded with the accompaniment of a rattle but the rhythm of the rattle is not clear. This song has a compass of an octave and moves freely within that compass. The phrases are only one measure in length and a rest does not occur in the song. The quadruple measure gives a "swing" to the rhythm of the song as a whole. Considering the subject of No. 201, the melody is particularly active. An ascent of a seventh occurs twice, and broken ascents and descents of a sixth are of frequent occurrence. The song is major in tonality and lacks the fourth and sixth tones of the complete octave. Progression is chiefly on the tones of a major triad. No. 202 is an active little melody which opens on the tones of a major triad and sixth but changes to a minor third, continuing that interval to the close of the song. The ritard to a slower tempo is coincident with the change to the minor third.

SONGS CONNECTED WITH TREATMENT OF THE SICK

The Seminole medicine man treats the sick with remedies revealed to him in dreams, these being nocturnal dreams and not visions induced by fasting. Some of these remedies are believed to act by their presence and are worn in little bags on the person. Thus a child, suffering from a cold, had several little bags of medicine around its neck, though it did not wear these at other times. A little bag of medicine was seen around the neck of a very small baby, and sometimes a large bag that would contain at least two cupfuls of herbs was seen hanging down a baby's back. In Charlie Dixie's camp a baby about 6 months old was seen with no clothing, but around its neck were two strings of beads and a medicine bag.

The Seminole sing when treating the sick, but the custom appears to differ in the Big Cypress and Cow Creek groups. Panther, a member of the former group, said the singing at such a time and when preparing medicines was not in "set melodies" but resembled Billie

Motlo's talking when relating the story of the two brothers. This was monotonous, with occasional high, nasal tones sliding downward, yet it could not be called a chant. The Cow Creek group, however, used certain definite melodies for certain ailments or conditions, several being presented (Nos. 203–207). Billie Stewart, of this group, said that his people sing when they dig medicinal roots and also put tobacco in the ground at that time.

Panther, of the Big Cypress group, said the medicine man "calls on the north, east, south, and west and asks them to help the sick person," offering the same petition when preparing his medicines. If Panther had been a "full medicine man" he could not have talked with this freedom. He had been asked to become such a medicine man but felt that he "could not spare the time." It would have prevented his work for white men and other activities, as a medicine man must spend much time in solitude and meditation. Yet he knows the old ways and often treats the sick. He became so interested in the present work that it seemed possible he would record his own medicine song, but he said that he "was afraid his medicine would not work next time" if he did so. Accordingly the request was not made, and the subject under consideration was changed. A similar policy has been followed in all tribes, and no medicine man has been asked to give information or do anything that would cause distress of mind at a future time.

Mrs. B. L. Lasher, wife of the owner of the Musa Isle Seminole Village, broke her ankle in 1930 and the Indians of the village offered their own form of treatment to help her. They were confident of success, and attributed her complete recovery to their aid. She did not know what they did in the camp but was aware that some actions were performed before they came to her room. In describing their actions in her room she said they burned about a cupful of leaves in a pan and carried it around the room for a few moments. The leaves had a peculiar odor and did not blaze. There was only a thin column of smoke from the middle of the leaves. One woman took some dry leaves from the edge of the pan and tucked them up under her blouse, and the men put some of the leaves inside their shirts.

On another occasion, during the same illness, they treated her for severe pain in her head. An old Indian came into the room, got a cup of hot water and made passes over it with his hands, and then motioned to her to drink the water. There was no perceptible taste. He talked during the entire treatment and was sure she would be relieved. She does not understand the language sufficiently to know what he was saying while he gave the treatment.

The principal singer for the sick in the Cow Creek group is Billie Smith, an old man living near Fort Drum. The writer went to his home, but he was absent. Fort Drum is about 20 miles north of Okeechobee, and the surrounding country is flat and treeless.

A remarkable series of songs was recorded by Susie Tiger, the wife of Billie Stewart, who uses them at the present time in treating the sick. Susie Tiger speaks even less English than her husband and understands only the simplest phrases. William King acted as interpreter. The songs for the sick are taught to children "as soon as they are old enough to appreciate them." Susie Tiger said that she had no songs to induce sleep. This question was asked as Indian doctors, in some tribes, seek first to quiet a patient.

Lumbago is an ailment that Susie Tiger treats with special success, and she recorded the song that she uses in her treatment. She sings this and "blows on the place where the pain is," repeating this four times. Then she lets the patient rest while she "makes a tea" which may be administered either internally or externally. The song was said to be "about the sand." Circumstances made it impossible to secure further information concerning the words or the remedy.

No. 203. Song used in treatment of lumbago

(Catalog No. 2273)

Recorded by SUSIE TIGER

The next song was sung for a sick baby. The idea of a dog that does not die is unique but, as always, the translation was written down in the words of the interpreter. At a later time the following sentence was noted in a translation of Homer's Odyssey: "Each side the porch stood figures of dogs ingeniously contrived by Hephaestus the crafts-man out of gold or silver, to be age-less, undying watch-dogs for this house of great-hearted Alcinous" (Homer, 1932, p. 96). It is recalled that colonists from Greece and adjacent islands were brought to northern Florida at an early date. It is not unusual to find traces of European fairy stories and Biblical narratives in Indian lore, and

No. 204. Song for a Sick Baby

Recorded by SUSIE TIGER

(Catalog No. 2277)

Translation.—The dog has no death. The sick baby is drinking from the dog that has no death.

the influence of these colonists may have extended farther and re-mained longer than has been supposed. A single idea, penetrating the mind of Indians with a scanty knowledge of the language, may be developed and applied in strange, native ways.

In connection with the three remaining songs used by Susie Tiger a peculiar procedure was followed. Before giving the decoction of medicine to the patient she "blew into it," by means of a reed (cf. p. 39). This reed is about 13 inches long and has a hole at one side, near one end. She inserts this end in the liquid and blows through it, so that the medicine "foams and bubbles." A similar custom was noted among the Alabama in Texas (Densmore, 1932) and described by a native of Santo Domingo Pueblo, New Mexico (Densmore, 1938, pp. 38, 40, 56, pl. 4). In that tribe the reed has a whistle opening that is partially covered by the index finger of the player's right hand. This controls the tone. The lower end is submerged in shallow water, in a bowl. "When the whistle is blown, the air passes down through the water, producing a pleasing, limpid sound supposed to resemble the singing of birds." This is used by members of the powerful Flint medicine society when treating the sick. It was said "the medicine men call in the birds and animals." Each medicine man has several of these whistles of various lengths, and a healing song was recorded with the words "The spirit birds and animals respond." Among the Seminole and Alabama the blowing of the breath of the medicine man or woman, through the water, was believed to make the medicine effective. The medicine used with the next song was a decoction of sassafras root.

No. 205. Song for bringing a child into the world

(Catalog No. 2276)

Recorded by SUSIE TIGER

Translation.

You day-sun, circling around,
You daylight, circling around,
You night-sun, circling around,
You poor body, circling around,
You wrinkled age, circling around,
You spotted with gray, circling around,
You wrinkled skin, circling around.

After singing this song she addresses the child, according to whether she thinks it is a boy or a girl, and says, "Boy, come," or "Girl, come." She then takes the reed and blows into the decoction, and gives it to the mother to drink.

When a sick person is near to death, Susie Tiger sings the two songs next following. The first song contains only the words "The white sun-lady," which were not explained. The Seminole usually refer to the sun as a man.

No. 206. "The White Sun-Lady"

(Catalog No. 2274)

Recorded by SUSIE TIGER

Part 1.

No. 206. "The White Sun-Lady"—Continued

After singing this song she blows into a decoction of ginseng [16] through a reed, as described in connection with the preceding song, and gives the medicine to the sick person to drink. This was said to "cool the sick person inside." This song and treatment represents the effort of the Indians to prolong life, although there is no reason to think the effort will be successful. An instance of this was observed among the Chippewa in 1907 (cf. Densmore, 1910, pp. 51–55).

Susie Tiger sings the next song for a person who is dying. The medicine is a decoction of ginseng, and the procedure is different from that in the preceding songs. She sings the song, blows into the medicine, and repeats the song until each action has been performed four times. Then the sick person drinks the medicine.

No. 207. Song for the Dying

Recorded by SUSIE TIGER

(Catalog No. 2275)

Translation.

Come back.
Before you get to the king tree, come back,
Before you get to the peach tree, come back,
Before you come to the line of fence, come back,
Before you get to the bushes, come back,
Before you get to the fork of the road, come back,
Before you get to the yard, come back,
Before you get to the door, come back,
Before you get to the fire, come back,
Before you get to the middle of the ladder, come back.

The song is addressed to the spirit that is about to depart.

In explanation of the first line of the words it was said that the king tree has large white blossoms and is the first tree to blossom in the spring. The other lines undoubtedly refer to various stages in

---

[16] "Ginseng, the root of a species of *Panax* (*P. ginseng*), native of Manchuria and Korea, belonging to the family Araliaceae, which is used in China as a medicine . . . The root is frequently forked, and it is probably due to this circumstance that medicinal properties were in the first place attributed to it, its resemblance to the body of a man being supposed to indicate that it could restore virile power to the aged and impotent . . . The action of the drug appears to be entirely psychic, and comparable to that of the mandrake of the Hebrews. There is no evidence that it possesses any pharmacological or therapeutic properties" (Ency. Brit. 1937 a, vol. 10, p. 359).

the journey of the spirit, such as have been described among the Winnebago, but circumstances made it impossible to ask further information (Densmore, MS.).

After the last word the doctor calls the sick person by name and says, "Come back, come back."

ANALYSES OF SONGS CONNECTED WITH TREATMENT OF THE SICK

No. 203 (Cat. No. 2273).—This unusual melody consists of four sections, three of which were repeated, the changes of tempo being given in all the renditions. These changes are probably connected with the words. About three-fourths of the intervals are minor thirds and whole tones. The interval between D and C was less than a semitone and was sung uniformly in all the renditions. The pitch level was gradually raised a whole tone during the performance.

No. 204 (Cat. No. 2277).—Seven renditions of this song were recorded, the transcription being from the latter part of the performance. The melody is rhythmic in character but contains no rhythmic unit. The phrases are unusually short and separated by rests. With two exceptions the intervals are minor thirds and whole tones.

No. 205 (Cat. No. 2276).—This is the only healing song recorded by Susie Tiger which contains a rhythmic unit. The tones are more nearly referable to a keynote than in her other healing songs although the third above the keynote occurs only on the unaccented portions of a measure. Many renditions were recorded, each containing the changes of tempo indicated in the transcription.

No. 206 (Cat. No. 2274).—A 2-minute phonograph cylinder was not long enough to record this entire song so it was recorded on two cylinders. The first cylinder contains the entire first section of the song and part of the second section. The second cylinder contains the last part of the first section and all the second section of the song. There was a brief pause between the sections in each recording. The song was sung without hesitation and was evidently clear in the mind of the singer. In connection with its use we note the occurrence of both stimulating and soothing phrases, and the *urging* phrase that appears in both sections with the increase in tempo. About three-fourths of the intervals are transcribed as minor thirds and whole tones, but the intonation of this singer was not clear and the transcription cannot show the tones with accuracy, neither is it necessary to do so in songs of this character. The characteristic phrase in the first section of the song consists of the tones F–E flat–C–B flat, the same intervals appearing in the second section as B flat–A flat–F–E flat. The same sequence of intervals occurs in three songs used in the treatment of the sick by Charles Wilson, a doctor of the Yuma tribe (Densmore, 1932 b, Nos. 40, 41, 42).

No. 207 (Cat. No. 2275).—The opening phrase of this song is a simple melodic phrase ending with an accented eighth note. This is followed by a few spoken words. The remainder of the melody consists of two phrases characterized by intervals of a fourth and differing in rhythm. Each rendition ends with an unaccented eighth note that carries the attention forward to the recurrence of the ascending fourth, in the repeated portion. The effect of this is dramatic, in connection with the purpose of the song.

SONGS FOR SUCCESS IN HUNTING

The night before starting on a hunting expedition the Seminole sing certain songs which are believed to make the animals "feed close in" and be more easily found by the hunters. The leaves of a plant known as "stingy man's tobacco" are put on the fire and the hunters hold their hands in the smoke and rub it on their faces and bodies; they also hold their guns, bags, and all their hunting equipment in the smoke. Some put the leaves in their pockets and some smoke it in their pipes together with native tobacco. Panther said, "If the boys are not having good luck they come to me or to Billie Motlo

No. 208. Song for success in hunting (a)

(Catalog No. 2110)

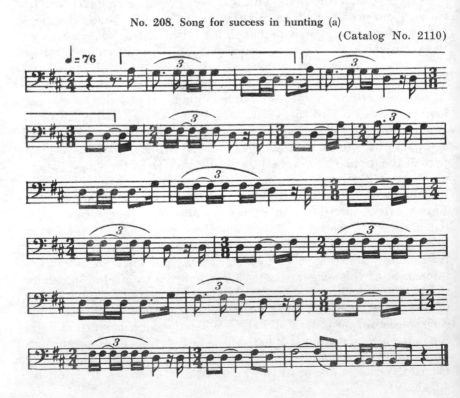

and get some of this stuff." [17]   He said the "stingy man's tobacco" was formerly used as a protective medicine in war and for safety when traveling in a canoe on rough water (cf. p. 29).

The songs for success in hunting are without accompaniment and are sung in succession, not in sets of four.   The leader sings the first phrase, then pauses while the men repeat the phrase, after which they all sing together.   In the first song this phrase probably consists of the first two measures.   A similar custom was heard in the songs of the Morning Star Ceremony of the Pawnee but is not a general custom among the Indians, the group usually joining the leader without a pause.   The Pawnee custom differed in that the leader sustained the last note of the opening phrase while the group sang it, thus approaching what is known as part singing (cf. Densmore, 1929 c, p. 20).

The characteristic ending of this class of songs is a downward glissando followed by a sound like clearing the throat, which cannot be indicated in notation.   We note that the Negro custom of "hollering" is often followed by a grunt.   The words of this song have no meaning.

All the songs of this series were recorded by Panther.

Panther said, "In the next song I talk about the bear, you know how it looks.   This makes him come into the swamp where the boys can see him."

No. 209. "It moves about as it feeds"

(Catalog No. 2111)

Translation (*describing the bear*).—Yellow nose, small eyes, round ears, dark body, big hind quarters, short tail.   It moves about as it feeds.

---

[17] Herbs were similarly used by other tribes to attract game.   (Cf. Densmore, 1928, p. 376; 1929 a, p. 110; 1932 a, p. 62.)

The words of the next song mention the old deer, the old bear, and the old gobbler.

No. 210. Song for success in hunting (b)

(Catalog No. 2112)

This appears to complete the song next preceding, as the only words are contained in the title.

No. 211. "They are feeding"

(Catalog No. 2113)

No. 212. "The old bear makes a noise"

(Catalog No. 2114)

Translation.—Old she-bear makes a noise [going through the brush]. She scares the little birds and they fly away with their noise.

In the next song the hunter complains of his bad luck.

No. 213. The Unsuccessful Hunter

(Catalog No. 2115)

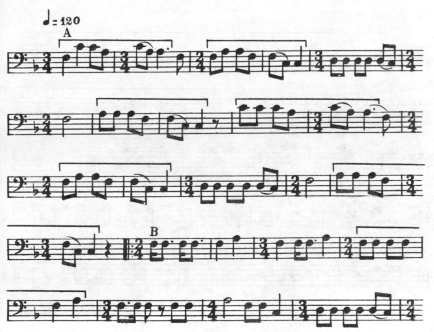

No. 213. The Unsuccessful Hunter—Continued

Translation.—My old people had deer-heads on the other side of the fire. That makes bad luck for me. I get nothing.

The three songs next following have the same melody with slight variations and different words.

No. 214. "We are going to hunt"

(Catalog No. 2116)

Free translation.—A long time ago two men, Ka lahali, had good luck all the time. They killed hundreds of deer every day. We are going to hunt.

A hunting custom of the Seminole was described by Panther who said, "When we hunt we trail game by its footprints. Sometimes one man goes around and we surround the game. The next song talks about how one man drives up the game for another."

"A man drives in the game"
Duplication (a) of No. 214

(Catalog No. 2117)

The title of the next song refers to the scaffold used for storing meat and kettles. The thought of an empty storage space would stimulate the hunter.

"The scaffold is empty"
Duplication (b) of No. 214

(Catalog No. 2118)

The Seminole "packs" the dead animal on his back. The forelegs are tied together and fastened to the man's shoulders, the middle of the animal is tied to the man's waist, and the animal's hind legs are tied together. In this manner the hunter carries home the game. The next song brings to the mind of the singer a picture of this action, which will incite him to action.

No. 215. "We are tying up the dead animal"

(Catalog No. 2119)

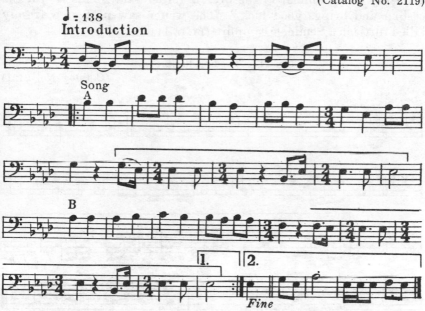

Translation.—We are tying up the dead animal. We tie its legs. We tie its body.

No. 216. Song for success in hunting (c)

(Catalog No. 2120)

Translation.—Fat game. We search for it.

The final song of the series refers to the custom of putting part of a freshly killed animal in the fire. Panther said, "This is still the custom and brings good luck." The writer saw part of a freshly killed turtle in a Seminole campfire (cf. p. 14).

No. 217. "Feeding the fire" (d)

(Catalog No. 2121)

Translation.—My grandfather [the fire] eats the deer's heart (the mulct).

ANALYSES OF SONGS FOR SUCCESS IN HUNTING

No. 208 (Cat. No. 2110).—The rhythm of this song was transcribed with difficulty. The rhythmic unit is not repeated with exactness though the divisions of its opening count are repeated approximately throughout the melody. The rests were given with distinctness. The implied keynote is D, but the third above that tone occurs only as a short, unaccented tone. Two renditions were recorded and are alike except for the omission of a few measures near the close of the second rendition. This may have been due to a fear lest the end of the phonograph cylinder be reached before the formal close of the song was given.

No. 209 (Cat. No. 2011).—This song contains the same tone material as the preceding and is similarly placed with reference to the keynote but is entirely different in other respects. It begins on the accented count of the measure, has a short, frequent rhythmic unit, and contains only one change of measure length. The compass of an octave is spanned several times, and a fourth is the most frequent progression. As in other songs with period formation, the second period is shorter and in a different rhythm from the first.

No. 210 (Cat. No. 2112).—Three consecutive renditions of this song were recorded and found to be identical in every respect. The third rendition was followed by the usual formal ending. Attention is directed to the rhythm of the song, comprising measures in 3–8, 4–8, 5–8, 6–8, and 7–8 time. These measure lengths were clearly indicated by the accented tones, and combine to form the rhythm of the melody as a whole.

No. 211 (Cat. No. 2113).—This melody contains the same tones as the song next preceding but has a rhythmic unit in 3–8 time, the repetitions of this unit being interrupted only by a few short phrases in a different time. The renditions of this song were recorded on two cylinders for comparison. The only differences occurred in measures containing words, which showed slight changes in note values. The performance was followed by the usual glissando phrases.

No. 212 (Cat. No. 2114).—The only tones in this song are those of the major triad and sixth. The melody moves freely, with a simple, flowing rhythm, and the song is particularly pleasing. After singing the song as transcribed there followed a repetition beginning with the seventh measure. The ascending and descending intervals are more nearly equal than in a majority of Indian songs, yet the general trend of each phrase is downward.

.No. 213 (Cat. No. 2115).—This interesting melody is in the period formation with the second period unusually long. The compass of this period is lower than that of the first, which is also unusual but it opens with the customary change of rhythm and measure length. Accented half notes are used effectively, and the rise and fall of the melody, with its simple but subtle rhythm, is in contrast with the songs of social dances.

No. 214 (Cat. No. 2116).—Two duplications of this song (Cat. Nos. 2117 and 2118) were recorded by the same singer, using different words. The singer regarded them as separate songs, in accordance with Indian custom, but a comparison shows them to be variants of the same melody. The pitch and tempo of the first and second "song" are the same, the third being lower and more rapid. The period formation is the same in all, the second period beginning on the same tone as the first. Differences in note values in the three renditions are due to differences in the words which were clearly pronounced.

No. 215 (Cat. No. 2119).—This song has a short introduction and consists of two periods. The intonation was not clear in the first period but the tones are transcribed as nearly as possible and comprise

a minor triad and seventh, the tones occurring in descending order.
The rest in the rhythmic unit was given with clearness and adds
interest to the phrase.

No. 216 (Cat. No. 2120).—The chief interest of this song is in its
rhythm. The unit is short and its consecutive occurrences are followed by measures in 3–4 and 7–8 time. Progression is chiefly by
major thirds and semitones, which is an unusual combination of
intervals.

No. 217 (Cat. No. 2121).—Three descending whole tones are prominent in the opening portion of this melody and are followed by the
descending fourth E–B, completing the compass of an octave. These
measures are followed by a brisk phrase on an ascending and descending major second and a closing measure in which a fourth is followed
by a minor third. The intonation was uncertain on the final measures
but the pitch is indicated as nearly as possible.

SONGS FOR SUCCESS IN THE BALL GAME

The legendary origin of the ball game among the Creeks was related by Billie Stewart and interpreted by William King, a Creek
from Oklahoma. The story is presented in the words of the
interpreter.

There was once a tribe called Calusa. They looked like Negroes and started
in the north—way up in Florida. These people had no "medicine" and no power,
but the Creeks were powerful with their medicine. The Calusa attacked the
Creeks and then the Creeks destroyed all the Calusa. When they destroyed
the Calusa they hoped to get something valuable from them, but didn't get
anything. There was one man of the Cheyenne tribe among the Creeks. He
went out in the woods and came back with two sticks fixed for ball-game sticks.
Our forefathers said they thought that God told him about those sticks. This
man brought the sticks to the Creeks and said, "Wouldn't it be a good thing for
us to make ball sticks to play with?" So they sat down and studied over it.
Everybody was happy about it and by means of this ball-stick game they got
the Stomp Dance. [The connection between the two was not explained.]

The interpreter said that the Creeks paint their faces with red
earth (pu kitca de) when they play ball and also in the Stomp Dance.
This was said to "make them look like giants and give good luck."
In the Creek tribe there were 25 men on a side. In the old days the
medicine man "made medicine" for their success. He had a buffalo
tail about a foot long and an inch wide, with the hair on it. The
players stood in a line. The medicine man sang and then blew into
the buffalo tail, inflating it. He laid this on the back of each player
and it "popped," making a sound that could be heard a long way.
It did not cause any sensation but made this sound. The player then
"scooted into the grass, turned a somersault, and went back to the

end of the line." When all had been treated in this manner they went to the ball ground. Each player had a tiger tail fastened at his belt attached at right angles to his body, and it bristled like a cat's tail when he played.

Billie Stewart said that the songs of the ball game were obtained from the Creeks and that his father used to sing them. It was the custom for the women to sing all the night before a game, and the men used a rattle and drum. The friends of one group of players danced in a long line, one behind another, the leader having a drum fastened to a strap over his shoulder. This was a water drum, consisting of a kettle containing water and having a buckskin top. It was beaten with the usual drumstick, about 10 inches long and wound with rags at the end. The people danced to bring success to their friends, and there was the betting that always accompanied Indian games. Many of these songs had words about success and defeating the opponents. Each song was followed by the form of "hallooing" peculiar to the game.

Sometimes the players wrestled before a game to test their strength, and sometimes they began the game at once. It was customary for the men of one town to play against the men of another town, and the friends of each side were there to watch the game, sometimes shouting encouragement to the players from their town or defying the opponents. Magic was used during the game and it was said, "If the ball is on the ground and the other side has stronger medicine they can make the ball invisible."

The following set of six songs, recorded by Billie Stewart, was sung during the night before a ball game by Seminole of the Cow Creek band.

No. 218. Ball Game Song (a)

(Catalog No. 2280)

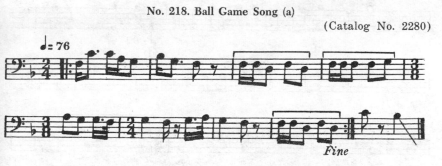

Translation.—You Talahasees are afraid to bet on yourselves.

No. 219. Ball Game Song (b)

(Catalog No. 2281)

Fine

No. 220. Ball Game Song (c)

(Catalog No. 2282)

Fine

Translation.—They are making fools of us and it is our fault.

No. 221. Ball Game Song (d)

(Catalog No. 2283)

Fine

No. 222. Ball Game Song (e)

(Catalog No. 2284)

Fine

No. 223. Ball Game Song (f)

(Catalog No. 2285)

The time of singing the next songs was not stated, but it was probably during the night before the game.

No. 224. Ball Game Song (g)

(Catalog No. 2293)

No. 225. Ball Game Song (h)

(Catalog No. 2294)

Fine

No. 226. Ball Game Song (i)

(Catalog No. 2295)

Fine

No. 227. Ball Game Song (j)

(Catalog No. 2296)

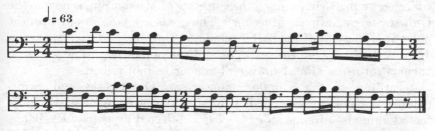

No. 228. Ball Game Song (k)

(Catalog No. 2297)

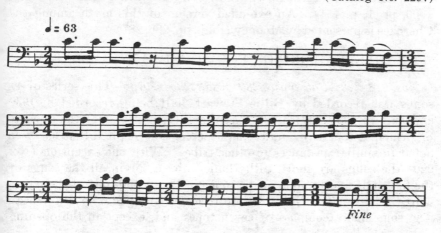

Fine

At the beginning of a game the ball was tossed into the air and caught by one man who threw it to another, after which the ball was "in play." The score was kept by means of 20 counters. Men hit one another freely with the ball sticks, and the game was a rough contest. The details of the game were not a subject of inquiry. It appears that each player held a racket ("stick") in each hand, as Culin states, "The game of ball with rackets . . . may be divided into two principal classes—first, those in which a single racket or bat is used; second, those in which two rackets are employed. The latter is peculiar to the southern tribes (Cherokee, Choctaw, Muskogee, Seminole), among whom the single racket is not recorded" (Culin, 1907, p. 562). The Choctaw, among whom this game was studied and its songs were recorded, use two rackets, the player holding one in each hand (Densmore, 1943 b). The implements of the game among the Seminole are described as follows by Culin: "Rackets and ball, the rackets (figure 777) saplings bent to form a scoop-shaped hoop, the ends lashed together for a handle, the hoop crossed by two thongs tied at right angles; the ball (figure 776), of two colors, one hemisphere light, the other dark, made of buckskin, with median seam; diameter, 2¾ inches" (Culin, 1907, p. 608). A similar specimen, collected by the writer among the Choctaw of Mississippi, is now in the United States National Museum. The goals are two sets of upright poles at either end of the ball ground and the object of each side is to drive its ball between the goal posts of the opponents. The game, in various forms, is almost universal among Indian tribes.

According to the Tuggle manuscript "The Creeks and Seminoles . . . have stories of ball games by the birds against the four-footed animals. In one story the bat is rejected by both sides, but is finally accepted by the four-footed animals on account of his having teeth, and enables them to win the victory from the birds" (Mooney, 1900, pt. 1, p. 454). An extended version of this myth among the Cherokee is presented by Mooney (ibid., pp. 286, 287).

ANALYSES OF SONGS FOR SUCCESS IN BALL GAME

Nos. 218–228 (Cat. Nos. 2280–2285, 2293–2297).—This series of 11 songs was recorded by Billie Stewart, half being recorded in 1932 and half in 1933. With two exceptions (Nos. 219, 221) the keynote or principal tone is F, indicating a perception of pitch that has been noted in similar instances in other tribes. With one exception (No. 220) the songs are short. Rhythmic units occur in all the songs of the first half and in none of the songs in the second half of the series. Three renditions of No. 218 were recorded and show no differences. The song has a compass of seven tones and, except in the opening measures, it progresses entirely by minor thirds and whole tones. The compass of No. 219 is the same as that of the preceding song and it contains similar descending intervals in the opening measures, but the implied tonality and general effect of the melody is different. This song contains two rhythmic units and their repetitions comprise the entire melody. The rhythm of No. 220 is unusually interesting, and the changes in tempo were clearly given. The first rhythmic unit is followed by two different phrases. The second unit contains the same count divisions with a different accent, followed by two eighth notes. The varied treatment of this short phrase gives coherence to the melody as a whole. The tones are those of the major triad and fourth. The next song (No. 221) also shows an interesting treatment of the rhythmic unit. This phrase ends with a 3–8 measure except in its first occurrence. All the phrases have a downward trend and the song contains all the tones of the octave except the seventh. The two songs next following (Nos. 222, 223) were said to be different songs but the melodies differ only in the latter portion. The pitch and tempo are the same and each was followed by shouts and downward glissando tones. The ending of the second song is the more interesting. The five songs next following were sung almost without a break in the time. None of these songs contains a rhythmic unit. The first song of this group (No. 224) is minor in tonality and based on the tones D–F–A–C, occurring chiefly in ascending progression. The same tones form the framework of No. 226 but the sequence is different and the song is major in tonality. The remaining songs of the series (Nos. 225, 226, 227, 228) have a compass of five or six tones and are simple melodies, without decided rhythms.

STORIES AND LEGENDS

THE OPOSSUM AND HER LOST BABY

Related by Panther

When Panther was a boy, 4 to 6 years of age, his father told him this story which is presented in practically his own words. John Billie, an old man, said that he also heard the song when he was a child.

An opossum had a little baby. She was going somewhere and carried the baby along, all the time.

The opossum found some wild potatoes and put the baby down while she dug the potatoes. She went away a little distance and every little while she called the baby, and it answered. [The narrator imitated the call and answer.] When the opossum came back she found that someone had stolen the baby and taken it away. The answer had come from a frog, put where the baby had been.

Then the opossum looked around and found somebody's tracks. She followed the tracks. She was lonesome and she sang a song. She sang it four times,

once with each of the stops that she made on her way to find the baby. There
is only one word in the song and that is I-ya-ta-wa-kits-ko-tic, which was the
baby's name.

No. 229. The opossum calls her lost baby

(Catalog No. 2139)

Recorded by PANTHER

She came to a house. Somebody was there and she asked if they had seen
anybody going by, carrying a baby. The person in the house said "Yes." The
opossum went in the direction they indicated and on the road she met two people
and asked them the same question. Then she had been to two places and met
two people, and sang her "lonesome song" twice.

After a while she came to another place. In that place the baby had been
hidden. There were four or five houses, some occupied and some empty. The
opossum asked her question and somebody pointed to a house saying, "They
got the baby in there." She went over, opened the door and found the baby
inside. Somebody had killed a rattlesnake, cooked it, and given it to the baby to
eat. The mother was angry and told them to take it away. She took the baby
and started home. She killed a little fawn, ate some of the meat, and gave some
to the baby. They stayed there a while. That made three times she sang the
song.

A wolf came to that place and smelled the meat. The opossum lied and said
she had no meat, but the wolf smelled the meat. The wolf got a bow and arrow.
Then the opossum was afraid she would be killed. She went up a big tree, took
the baby with her and stayed up in the top of the tree. The baby died up there
in the tree. That was the fourth time she sang the song.

The old opossum came down and walked away. She found a skunk who was
her friend and went home with the skunk. They lay down together and sang.
They sang another "lonesome song" and then they both died. This is the last song.

No. 230. The opossum dies

(Catalog No. 2140)

Recorded by PANTHER

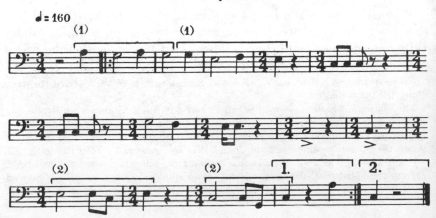

WHY THE RABBIT IS WILD

Related by Panther

The following story was related by Panther.

At first the Indians were under the ground, in a big hole, then they all came out. When they came out they bathed in a little creek. When they got through bathing they had nothing to eat and no fire.

One man told them what to do and how to make a fire. He told them to take dry, soft bark, twirl a stick between their hands, and then a spark lighted the bark. He got some dry punk. One man made the spark, another caught it on the punk, then they made a fire, but they had no pots or kettles.

The man heard a noise a half a mile or so toward the north. He thought some animals were there. He sent two men to get little trees and out of these he made bows and arrows. He got ready, then sent the boys and men to find something to eat.

They found deer, turkey, and bear and brought them back to camp. Then they had plenty of meat but nothing else. The man tried to find something else and found swamp cabbage. He cut it down and told the people to eat it raw, as they had no kettles. Then he taught them to roast it in the ashes of a fire.

The two men talked it over. One man had made the bows and arrows and the other had taught them to roast the swamp cabbage and to cook meat in the same way, putting some in the fire. One man said to the other, "What shall we live in?" They had been sleeping in the grass. So they made themselves a house, like those the Seminole live in now. Then a horse and dog talked to the man, talking like people. At that time the rabbit stayed with people and he told lies all the time, but the dog and horse told the truth.

Somebody found out that the rabbit lied. Then the rabbit tried to do something all the time. He would go away, and when he came back he would say he had seen things that he had not seen. He would say he had seen snakes, alligators, and turtles.

The man said to the rabbit, "If you find a snake, kill him and bring him back to camp." The rabbit killed a snake and brought it to the camp, and he sang a song with words that meant "On his back." [The word *Co* was said to mean "back." The meaning of the following words or syllables has not been ascertained—Co kco ita a ho pi tli tci yca na nac.]

No. 231. The rabbit brings back a snake

(Catalog No. 2138)

Recorded by PANTHER

When the rabbit was bringing back the snake he saw an alligator. The man said, "You kill the alligator and bring him back." The alligator talked, too, at that time. The rabbit said, "Somebody wants to see you up at the camp." The alligator believed this and went along with the rabbit. When they had gone about halfway the rabbit tried to kill the alligator; he beat the alligator but could not kill him and the alligator went back to his cave.

Then the rabbit came home.

The man said, "If you see a turkey, kill him and bring him home." So the rabbit started out to get a turkey, but he went to a wildcat and said, "You kill a turkey for me." Wildcat went and found a turkey and killed him. Rabbit brought the turkey back to camp and told the man that he had killed it. The man believed it.

Then the rabbit wanted to get married. The man thought the rabbit had killed the turkey and given it to the girl. But when rabbit got married he didn't bring any food at all. The people found out that the rabbit did not kill the turkey, so they drove the rabbit away from the camp. That is why the rabbit is wild today.

THE RABBIT WHO STOLE THE FIRE

Related by Billie Stewart and interpreted by William King

The people were having a Stomp Dance. Rabbit was a great singer and leader so they let him lead. Twice he ran up to the fire and made signs. The people thought he was wonderful. The third time he picked up a brand from the fire and ran toward the woods. He ran so fast that the people could not catch him, so they made medicine for rain to put out the fire.

When Rabbit came back, some people said, "Do not let him lead again as he steals the fire." Others said, "Don't let us be stingy." So they let him lead and he picked up a firebrand as before. They made medicine for rain again and it put out the fire.

Rabbit came back. Some said, "Don't let him lead again," but he had some friends who got him to lead. The same thing happened right over. But Rabbit found a hollow rock out in the woods. He could get in this hollow and keep the rain from putting out the fire. He rubbed some sort of oil on his hair, for he was afraid it might catch fire.

They let him lead again, and this time he went up toward the fire and stuck out his head. His hair caught fire and he ran out. The people ran after him but could not catch him, so they made another rain, but he had gone into the hollow rock that he had prepared. It rained and rained but he was safe.

He came out once in a while and set fire to grass but the people made rain and put it out. He did this four times and then they never saw any more fire. They thought Rabbit was finished up but he still had some fire, so he got out of the rock and got into the ocean, carrying the fire and intending to swim across.

The people saw the smoke across the ocean and knew that Rabbit had carried the fire across and spread it out. They were angry at him but couldn't reach him.

That is the way that everybody got fire.

William King, after interpreting this story, stated that in his grandfather's version of the story, the rabbit came from the other side of the ocean to this side, reversing the action of this story. He also said that his father "got fire by firing into cotton with his rifle."

LEGEND CONCERNING THE DOG

The dog spoke like people and he took care of the baby. One day the dog didn't want to take care of the baby and the dog said, "See my paws." Then the man made the dog's paws as they are now, and the dog could not talk any more. After that *none* of the animals could talk any more, but the Indians continued to talk. Sometimes an Indian did not tell the truth, and the rabbit found it out. Then the rabbit stayed wild.

This happened before the high water killed all the people.

The old men, not the women, told the stories to children. Food and tobacco were taken to an old man with a request that he tell such stories as those which follow.

THE ORIGIN OF WHITE CORN

Related by Susie Tiger and interpreted by William King

The Seminole always refer to themselves as "A jia tki," which means *white corn,* and in the beginning they were white people.

An old woman was living with her grandchild. She made good *sofki* for the boy and it tasted good to him. He would go out and hunt, kill game and bring it to this grandmother. They all ate together, drank *sofki* and ate deer meat.

The boy did not know how his grandmother got the corn to make the *sofki.* He wanted to know where she got the corn, and he told his grandmother that he was going hunting again. Instead of going, he sneaked back to watch her make the *sofki.* He saw her go into a shack and sit down. She had very sore ankles that were so very dry that she could scrape off the flakes of skin. The boy watched her scrape off the flakes and bring them into the house. She got the pot and some water and put the flakes in the water. The boy found out that the *sofki* came from his grandmother's sore ankles.

After that he would not drink the *sofki.* His grandmother said, "Why don't you drink *sofki*?" He did not explain because he knew where it came from. The grandmother suspected that the boy had watched her, so she asked him, "Did you watch me doing something?" The boy did not reply, but said he would not drink *sofki* any more.

His grandmother told him that he must burn their house and everything. The reason was that the boy had found out her secret and she did not want to live any more. She told the boy to tell the people to burn the house over her, while she was in it.

A few days after the house was burned they came to see the ruins and found the old house restored and full of corn. From there the corn spread over all the earth.

That is the end of the story.

LEGEND OF THE FLOOD

Related by Panther

The earth was all covered with water, but before this happened a man made a big houseboat and many people stayed in it.

After a while the bass dived down and brought up earth in his mouth—maybe a handful. The man asked the bass to make land for the people but he said, "No, I just got that in my mouth." So the man made that earth into a ball.

The man was holding the ball and the beaver cut it in two with his tail. The man threw half toward the north and he threw the other half toward the south. The beaver made them into big countries, and the one toward the south was made into Cuba.

The man said, "Everybody stay inside 4 days and then the land will be dry." After 2 days the ivorybill wanted to get out and it got out. The buzzard wanted to get out too. These two came out. These birds still keep away from

people. The dogs stayed with the people, as they do now, and the people stayed
in the big houseboat 4 days. After 4 days the man let them all out. By that time
a big country was dry and it was a good country.

LEGEND CONCERNING THE TWO BROTHERS

Two versions of this story were recorded, one by a member of the
Everglades group and the other by a member of the Cow Creek group.
There was also an incomplete version by a man from the Everglades
group who was not qualified to tell the story in detail.[18]

CYPRESS SWAMP VERSION

The version first presented is that from the Everglades, related by
Billie Motlo (pl. 2, *a*, and p. 169), an old man who has the right to tell
the story. He related it in a monotonous tone, with occasional high,
nasal tones sliding downward. When Panther was discussing the
singing for the sick he said it resembled Billie Motlo's talking, when
relating this story. Panther acted as interpreter for Billie Motlo,
and the story is presented in his words. Attention is directed to the
style and rhythm which are reminiscent of the Bible. The adapta-
tion of Bible teachings to Seminole history and environment is evident throughout the narrative. In old times, if such a story was to
be told in the evening, those who intended to listen ate nothing "after
the sun was halfway up the sky," this being at about 10 o'clock in the
morning. It was said, "they remember better if they have not eaten
during the day."

In the beginning there were two brothers. They were gods and their father
and mother lived in the sky. These two brothers were small, and afterward
the people grew larger and were the same size as the people of today.

The oldest of these brothers worked in the field and the younger brother had
sheep. The older brother got plenty of food from his field, but the younger
brother fought and killed him, burying him. When he was ready to bury his
brother their mother called him, but he did not go. He stayed at that place.
The next morning he went to his mother and told her and his father that he
had killed his brother and buried him.

After that, perhaps 3 years afterward, someone tried to kill him. Then his
father and mother went up and tried to take him along. He did not want to go.
He wanted to stay with his own people. About a year later the Spanish people
tried to beat him. They nailed his hands and feet but could not kill him. He
got away to two or three different places and tried to make (get) home but they
found him and tried to beat him to death. Every time he moved to a new place.

He found one family and asked the man of that family what he *did*. The man
said, "I plant rocks." [He said this as a joke.] The man went 5 or 6 miles

---

[18] Dr. J. R. Swanton states, in correspondence, that this story is "a somewhat attenuated
version of the 'Lodge Boy and Thrown Away' story which is widely spread among Indian
tribes . . . Mooney gives a Cherokee version and similar stories have been collected from
the Shoshoni, Crow, Blackfoot, Hidatsa, Gros Ventres, Arapaho, Wichita, Omaha, Sauk and
Fox, Kickapoo, Assiniboin, Pawnee, Menominee, Ojibwa, Micmac, Iroquois, Kiowa, Tsim-
shian and Netwetee, though of course it undergoes considerable changes in such a wide
area of distribution." (Cf. Swanton, 1929, p. 270.) The same authority presents two
Natchez versions, one Alabama, and one Creek version of this story.

farther and found a very poor family [Seminole] that had a little camp to raise their food. Those people gave him food and drink and told him to sit down and rest. They told him to make a garden for himself. The man of the family asked him how large a garden he wanted to make and what he wanted to plant, and went with him to help him make the garden. They looked at the land and then went back to the camp, and the people gave him a good supper and let him sleep inside the grass house. The man and his family slept outside. In every way they were good to this poor stranger who had nothing.

About midnight the man, who was outside with his family, awoke and heard a lot of noises of hogs, horses, sheep, chickens, and colts eating. He went to sleep again. When he woke in the morning he was in a good bed, in a good house—a *big* house. Outside were all kinds of animals—a mule and all animals. He got up and opened the door.

The man to whom he had given his own house woke up, and showed him how to take *care* of those animals. There was corn and oats in the field and he showed the man how to feed it to the animals.

The women cooked their breakfast and then they went to look at the land again. Everything had grown—pumpkins, corn, beans, sweetpotatoes—all had grown in the night.

Then the stranger said, "I will stay with you one day, then I go away tomorrow. Somebody may follow my track, sometime, and ask you, 'Did you see a man? How did you get these animals and vegetables?' Do not *tell* him."

Then the stranger went away 200 or 300 miles, going south. He came to a place all water, no land. He made himself a three-masted ship, made it in a minute. He crossed the big water and went to another country.

About 40 people [Spanish] followed his track and found his first camp. They asked how a certain man looked and the people *told*. They came to the camp where he made the animals and asked the same questions, but that man didn't tell anything. He said he just raised the vegetables and animals. But they [the Spaniards] saw the tracks and followed. When they got to the big water the tracks ended, but they made a boat so as to follow the man. He left a note telling how to make the boat and these people found the note and made the boat that day. They finished the boat in one week.

Then the 40 people went across the water and found the man. They put the man on the boat and brought him back. They beat him and tried to kill him but they could not do so. The man got tired of it and said, "If you want to kill me, get a knife, get a blind woman to cut out my heart and that will kill me." The blind woman took the knife, stuck it into him, cut out his heart, and blood gushed out. The blood struck the blind woman's eyes and she could see. When she saw what she had done she cried, but it did not do any good.

The 40 people were glad the man was killed. He was buried. Four days afterward, in the morning, he got up, and went up into the air. Somebody heard a lot of chickens, a little rooster, and a little Fido-dog making a noise high up in the air. When they looked up, they saw the man's body going up in the air.

The man's mother and father lived up there. He went all that day and about sunset he got to the place where his mother and father lived. He went to his parents' house and knocked. His mother opened the door. The man was covered with blood. His father was angry when he saw this. He went to the corner and got his big machete and said he was going to kill all those wicked people.

The man said, "The English and all the other people were good. It was only the Spanish who killed me."

There was a Spanish city, and it was cut in two and half of it was sunk in the mud. The man's father thought the people were killed, but they had a city under the water and lived there.

This is the story of the beginning of people.

An incomplete version from the same group stated that, long ago, there were twins among the Seminole, one good and the other bad. The good twin made all the animals and gave the Indians "hunting medicine" and bows and arrows by which they could secure the animals for food. The bad twin "was responsible for whatever bad luck came to the Indians."

COW CREEK VERSION

Billie Stewart related the version of this story from the Cow Creek group, William King acting as interpreter. Stewart said:

My father once told me there was a woman and man who had lived together and then separated for a long time. The man went away and came back. Certain parties told them they ought to get together again and they did. They had two children—twin boys. One went down the road and turned into a mouse. The other saw it and wanted to catch it. He asked his mother to help him catch it. They caught the mouse.

These twins were foolish and always in mischief. They killed their grandfather who was sick and lying on the floor. They cut a piece of flesh from his thigh and roasted it. They saved it. The grandmother had gone away and they waited for her to come back. They did everything with one accord and so when they roasted this flesh they agreed to tell their grandmother that they had killed a gray squirrel for her.

When she came back they got the meat, told their story and she ate the meat. The twins were all doubled up with laughter and sang a song with the words "she is eating grandpa's flesh."

After two or three times she "caught on to it." She knew they were going too far with their deviltry, so she decided they would have to be killed. Some men were talking under an arbor and she went over and told them to kill the twins. They [the twins] knew her thoughts so they went over there to listen. One sat by their father, but the boy had become a flower which stood blooming beside him. The father thought it was a flower, picked it and started toward the fire. He threw it toward the fire and it turned into a bird and went up in the air.

The other boy had turned into a crow, sitting on a tree. He went up in the air and they both went to a house. They had a gourd with a hole in it, and put into it everything that would sting—ants, wasps, and so forth. The people who were going to kill them saw the twins go into the house. They went in, but the twins had the gourd full of stinging things and they broke it, so the things flew out. The stinging things killed some people and the others scattered.

When the twins went outside they said, "Perhaps our father is lying here somewhere." They found him dead.

One twin had a bow and se-sawed it across his father's leg and the father turned into a crow and went up in the air. The boys went up in the air also and each twin became a thunder which you hear before a rain. The thunder is the twin boys. That is the end of the story.

Mr. King, adding to the story he had translated, said he heard that the bad boy went toward the west and the good boy went toward the east. The boy who went west said, "When you see a red cloud remember me." He was the storm. The other boy said, "When you see lightning remember me. I bring good weather."

The people lay very still during the telling of a story. There is an old saying "If everybody does not spit after a man has told a story they will get hump-shouldered."

MISCELLANEOUS SONGS

The removal of the Seminole to Oklahoma took place in 1836–40. Two songs concerning that event were recorded.

No. 232. Song concerning the removal of the Seminole to Oklahoma (a)

Recorded by SUSIE TIGER

(Catalog No. 2278)

Translation.
They are taking us beyond Miami,
They are taking us beyond the Caloosa River,
They are taking us to the end of our tribe.
They are taking us to Palm Beach, coming back
　　beside Okeechobee Lake,
They are taking us to an old town in the west.

It was said the Seminole sang the next song when on their way to Arkansas, which was a stopping place on their journey to Oklahoma.

No. 233. Song concerning the removal of the Seminole to Oklahoma (b)

(Catalog No. 2279)

Recorded by BILLIE STEWART

Translation.
We are going with [George] Washington.
Which boat do we get in?

The Seminole Indians once had Negro slaves. These were Negroes who ran away and joined the Indians, who refused to surrender them to their masters. This is said to have been one of the differences that led to the Seminole war. The words of the following song show it preceded the war which ended in 1842.

No. 234. "My old slaves"

Recorded by SUSIE TIGER

(Catalog No. 2450)

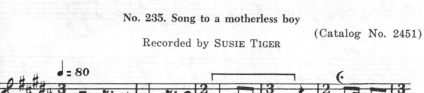

Translation.—My old slaves saddled my horse and stayed there all night.

It is regretted that no explanation was obtained concerning the words of this and the song next following except that the mother of the little boy was dead.

No. 235. Song to a motherless boy

Recorded by SUSIE TIGER

(Catalog No. 2451)

No. 235. Song to a motherless boy—Continued.

Translation.

Sleep well,
Your mother has gone to get a long turtle,
Little boy, go to sleep,
That is what your mother said.

No. 236. Song to a little child

(Catalog No. 2452)

Recorded by SUSIE TIGER

Translation.

Sleep, little girl,
Your mother has gone to the black prairie to hunt
    for the gopher turtle but she will return.
Sleep well. Sleep on.

The next three songs were said to be "sung while drinking" and are not connected with any dance. All were recorded by Susie Tiger.

No. 237. Drinking Song (a)

(Catalog No. 2453)

The next was said to be an old song.

No. 238. Drinking Song (b)

(Catalog No. 2454)

Translation.—I met my friend and we got to drinking a little too much.

No. 239. Drinking Song (c)

(Catalog No. 2455)

*singing
continued*

The four songs next following were recorded by Panther who said, "If I were going to see a Cow Creek man I would sing these four songs before I leave home." He said further that a long time ago a Seminole chief went to a soldier's camp carrying a flag and the soldier who met him also carried a flag. For that reason the songs are sometimes called "Flag songs." They are not used for dancing and anyone who wishes can sing them. The words of the first were translated "Come on here," and the second, "Come on everybody." The last two songs have no words.

No. 240. Song of friendship (a)

(Catalog No. 2141)

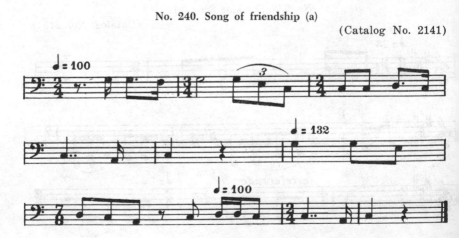

No. 241. Song of friendship (b)

(Catalog No. 2142)

No. 242. Song of friendship (c)

(Catalog No. 2143)

No. 243. Song of friendship (d)

(Catalog No. 2144)

ANALYSES OF SONGS WITH STORIES AND MISCELLANEOUS SONGS

No. 229 (Cat. No. 2139).—Four renditions of this song were recorded, each corresponding to an episode in the search for the opossum's baby (cf. p. 193). After the second rendition the singer paused and told the first and second episodes, saying the opossum went to two places and inquired of two people whom she met on the way, and that she sang the song calling for her lost baby in each instance. Then she sang the song twice, these renditions corresponding to the third and fourth episodes in the search. In the second pair of renditions the third measure was slightly changed by singing the third note as E and connecting it with the preceding tone, a change which may have been connected with a change in the words. The melody has a compass of eight tones and lies partly above and partly below the keynote.

No. 230 (Cat. No. 2140).—This song consists of two sections separated by exclamatory repetitions of the tone C. The second occurrence of this tone is particularly emphatic, with a syllable resembling *boom*. The rhythmic units at the close have an interesting effect of finality.

No. 231 (Cat. No. 2138).—The tone material of this song is the second 5-toned scale but the framework of the melody consists of two descending tetrachords and a succession of minor thirds. The triple time in the sixth measure gives an interesting effect of hesitation. Several renditions were recorded, and the pitch was a semitone lower than the transcription.

No. 232 (Cat. No. 2278).—Two renditions of this song were recorded, separated by a short pause. The transcription is from the first rendition, during which the pitch was raised a semitone. The transcription is on the pitch of the opening measures. The second rendition contained another rise of a semitone in the pitch level. The repeated portion began and ended as transcribed but contained some unimportant changes in the rendition. The incomplete occurrences of the rhythmic unit are interesting and unusual. A large majority of the intervals are minor thirds and whole tones. The melody contains all the tones of the octave except the seventh.

No. 233 (Cat. No. 2279).—This interesting melody has a compass of five tones and contains four periods, each with a slightly different rhythm, although the rhythmic unit occurs in each. It would be interesting to know what words occur with this little phrase that recurs like a thought that cannot be dispelled. The most prominent interval is the major third between G and B. The "swallowing of tones," indicated by ×, is described on page 215.

No. 234 (Cat. No. 2450).—The framework of this melody consists of two descending, overlapping tetrachords and repetitions of a minor third, with repetitions of the tone F which comprise four measures.

This is an unusual formation. The song contains measures in 3–8; 5–8, 2–4, 3–4, and 4–4 time and the tempo changes to a more rapid and then to a slower beat. Unimportant changes occurred in repetitions of the song.

Nos. 235, 236 (Cat. Nos. 2451, 2452).—The purpose of both these songs was to put a child to sleep, and the melodies resemble each other in containing short, descending phrases and an accelerated tempo leading to the same speed. The first song is a typical Indian melody of this class. The pitch level was raised a semitone during the second song.

Nos. 237–239 (Cat. Nos. 2453–2455).—These songs are minor in tonality and contain no rhythmic unit. No. 237 is a simple melody with a compass of five tones, repeating the triad with the fourth usually as a passing tone. The time is sharply increased and the new tempo continued to the end of the song. No. 238 also contains an accelerando, leading to the same tempo as in the preceding song. This melody has the unusual compass of 12 tones, the lowest tone being E, third space on the bass staff. The voices of Indian women are usually in a low register but rarely reach to this pitch. The song proceeds from the highest to the lowest tone of the compass in the first four measures and contains smaller count divisions than the other songs of this group. No. 239 is a simple melody with a compass of seven tones and frequent changes of measure lengths. The intervals comprise 13 ascending and 16 descending progressions.

Nos. 240–243 (Cat. Nos. 2141–2144).—The rhythm of these songs is different from the rhythm of the songs used with dancing. Nos. 240 and 241 begin with the same phrase, and open and close in the same tempo. The descending phrases are somewhat similar in the two songs but each melody is individual and was repeated several times. No. 240 is framed on the descending tones of a minor triad and minor seventh, comprising two overlapping triads, while No. 241 is framed on two descending, overlapping tetrachords which occur consecutively in the fifth measure. The first portion of No. 242 consists of the tones of a major triad with the second as a passing tone, and the song closes with repetitions of the keynote and the minor third below. The rhythmic unit occurs four times and is followed by a descent of a minor third in each occurrence, this being in varied rhythms. More than half the progressions are minor thirds. In No. 243 the tone material and melodic path resemble the song next preceding but the rhythmic treatment of the melody is different. The contrast between the two rhythmic units is interesting, the first beginning on an accented and the second on an unaccented tone, while the first interval of each is an ascending fifth. The proportion of minor thirds is about the same as in the preceding song.

SUMMARY OF ANALYSES OF SEMINOLE SONGS, WITH COMPARISONS BETWEEN SEMINOLE SONGS AND SONGS OF OTHER TRIBES

Tabulated analyses of individual songs, according to classifications in previous books, as well as the descriptive analyses already presented, are the basis for the following summary. This is presented under the following headings: tone material, melodic framework, melodic and rhythmic form, period formation, rise in pitch level, introductory phrases, connective phrases, use of the labial *m*, absence of accompaniment, formal and customary endings, indeterminate ending, ending on tone above keynote, and changes of a melody in its repetitions, "word swallowing," and forcible inhaling of breath.

Tone material.—This observation is based on the tones occurring in a song which are referable to a keynote, songs lacking in a keynote being classified as irregular in tonality. The 5-toned scales according to Helmholtz (1885, pp. 260, 261) have been noted in songs of other Indian tribes, the most frequent being the fourth 5-toned scale (major). This may be regarded as a major triad with the second and sixth added or it may be regarded as lacking the fourth and seventh tones of the complete octave. Examples in this series are Nos. 19, 22, 45, 53, 92, 98, 139, 142, 154, and 192. The tones of the second 5-toned scale (minor) lacking the second and sixth occur in Nos. 60 and 231, and the first 5-toned scale, lacking the third and seventh tones of the complete octave occur in Nos. 20, 21, 62, and 141.

Melodic framework.—The sequence of tones in a melody and their accents determine its framework. The simplest framework of a song with a compass of five or more tones is a major triad. If the compass is sufficiently extended these tones represent the upper partials, or overtones, of the fundamental. The triad may have passing tones, but is readily recognized as the framework of Nos. 170, 174, 180, 182–187, 190, 201, 202, 212, 220, 237, and 242. A melody may descend to the minor third below the keynote, this tone, with the keynote and the third, producing a minor triad. This framework is known as a minor triad with minor seventh and the tones generally occur in descending order. It may also be regarded as two overlapping triads, the upper being major and the lower being minor. This characterizes at least 13 Seminole songs and is mentioned in the analyses. This framework has been noted in other Indian tribes and among other primitive peoples, and was noted by early students of primitive music. Prof. J. C. Fillmore, who transcribed the Indian songs recorded by Alice C. Fletcher, found this among the Dahomey songs collected at the World's Columbian Exposition in 1893, and H. E. Krehbiel (in a paper read before the Folk-Lore Congress, July

1894) cited similar instances among the songs of the American Negroes. It occurred also in a song that Professor Fillmore recorded from Indians living on the Nass River in British Columbia. Many Seminole songs are framed upon overlapping tetrachords or contain such sequences. The tetrachord was prominent in the formation of songs recorded at Neah Bay, Wash. (cf. Densmore, 1939, pp. 44, 45).

Melodic and rhythmic form.—The simplest form of an Indian song is that in which the song as a whole is a unit and its repetitions constitute a larger unit. Thus it is sometimes difficult for an Indian to think of one rendition of a song as a unit, for he is accustomed to the cumulative effect of the song when in use. Another form is that in which the melody consists of four phrases, equal in length, the rhythm and perhaps the melodic characteristic being the same in the first, second, and fourth and different in the third phrase. This was noted with clearness in two Seminole songs (Nos. 65, 130) but occurs more frequently in songs recorded in the Middle West where the Indians have been in contact with Protestant missions and may have been influenced by the form of hymns. It was noted especially in songs of the Ghost Dance. The short phrases designated as rhythmic units occur in 114 Seminole songs, these constituting less than half the number. One or more rhythmic units occur in about 64 percent of 1,553 songs of 10 tribes, in a combined analysis (Densmore, 1939, p. 41).

Period formation.—Songs with this formation consist of two to four periods, or sections, designated by letters of the alphabet. Examples are Nos. 8, 9, 11, 25, 35, 78, 81, 85, 128, 209, 214 (and duplications) 215, and 233. It is interesting to note that 11 of these songs were from the Cypress Swamp group, only two were from the Cow Creek group, and one was attributed to the Calusa. This form was noted first in the songs of the Tule Indians from San Blas, Panama (Densmore, 1926, pp. 16, 34), and later was found in Yuman songs (Densmore, 1932 b, pp. 18, 19), and in a large number of songs of Acoma, Isleta, and Cochiti Pueblo songs (Densmore, 1957). It also occurred in a few very old Choctaw songs (Densmore, 1943 b). Among the Seminole it occurs more frequently in songs of the Cypress Swamp group than in songs of the Cow Creek group. An introduction characterizes these songs among the Pueblo but occurs seldom in Seminole songs. In all tribes, the first period (A) is the longest and its form suggests there may be some freedom in it. The second period (B) is shorter, in a different rhythm, and generally in a faster tempo. In other tribes it is higher in pitch, but in the Seminole songs it is usually in the same register as the first period. This may be followed by a repetition of the first period, or by a third and fourth period. Considerable freedom was noted in repetitions of all except the second period which was always sung alike in all renditions. An inquiry was made of Panther concerning this form of song and he recognized it at once. He said that in a complete rendition of the song there is a "different singing," then the previous "singing" is repeated. This would describe the period formation, the first period being regarded as the actual song. He said that the first and third sections may be of any length, but the second is always short and sung without change in repetitions. Panther readily designated the songs that "had different singing in the middle" and they were songs in the period formation.

Rise in pitch level.—This peculiarity occurs in songs with period formation, the rise being a semitone in the first period and, in one instance, another rise of a semitone later in the song. The transcription is on the pitch of the opening measures, and the higher pitch level was maintained to the close of the song. The examples in the present series are Nos. 78, 81, 85, 137, and 138 recorded by Panther, and Nos. 203, 232, and 236 recorded by Susie Tiger. The same peculiarity was noted in Pueblo songs with the period formation. The singer from Santo Domingo Pueblo said that his grandfather, who taught him the songs, also taught him to raise the pitch, stating this should be done in old war songs. In certain other classes of songs the pitch was lowered. A change in pitch level is a Japanese custom, an authority on the subject stating that "Songs in which the pitch is raised a semitone, after which the pitch level is sustained to the end of the song, is one of the peculiarities of ancient Japanese music. However, this type of music is quite exceptional and rare, and we can see such expressions only in the music called 'Rin-yu-Ga-Ku,' which was originally brought to Japan from India in the seventh century by the priests of Annam (China)." (Cf. Densmore, 1938, pp. 53–54.) A rise in pitch has also been noted in West Africa. T. E. Bowdich describes a stringed instrument, played with both hands, as an accompaniment to the reciting of long stories and "mentions two songs played with this instrument; one commences, he imagines, in F major and ends in G major" (Bowdich, as cited in Sadler, 1935, p. 75).

Introductory phrases.—This custom was noted in Pueblo songs and, as in those songs, the introductory phrases in Seminole songs appear to be somewhat indefinite in length. As a phonograph cylinder is short, the Indian was not encouraged to record all of such introductions, and a full discussion of that subject would detract his attention from the songs, which are more important. In some instances it is uncertain whether a monotonous phrase at the beginning of a transcription is the opening of the song or a short introduction. In six instances (Nos. 1, 57, 78, 153, 215, 207) the opening phrase appears to be an introduction and is so indicated. Similar instances were noted among the Makah. No. 4 entitled "Song to make a wounded whale swim toward shore," contained an introduction and also glissando cries (Densmore, 1939, p. 60).

Connective phrases.—In a large majority of Indian songs a repetition follows without a pause or connective phrase. In the Seminole songs such a phrase often resembles the glissando phrases that are sung after a song and seem rather indefinite in length. A short connective phrase is transcribed with Nos. 5, 22, 23, 125, 154, 155.

Use of the labial m.—This labial is not part of a word but a sound produced with lips closed and continuing for about the length of a quarter note. It occurs in three songs of the present series (Nos. 25, 103, 237). Two are songs of the Cow Creek group and one, recorded by a member of that group, was attributed to the Calusa, this being No. 25. It is interesting to note this connection with the northern region as other peculiarities were noted chiefly in the southern or Cypress Swamp group (cf. rise in pitch, pp. 208, 209). The labial *m* was heard in a few Choctaw songs recorded in Mississippi (Densmore, 1943 b), and was noted in five songs recorded at Neah Bay, Wash. (cf. Densmore, 1939, p. 95). The first of these instances occurred in the "Dream song of a whaler," recorded by an old medicine man of the Makah, and said to have been received in a dream. The others, recorded by the same man, were connected with dreams or the healing of the sick. It was also used as a sign of endearment between a mother or grandmother and a small child (ibid., p. 277). This labial is a Negro custom and may have been carried to Neah Bay by Negroes or members of a party of Spaniards who visited that village many years ago.

Absence of accompaniment.—Two classes of Seminole songs were sung without accompaniment, these being the songs of the Snake Dance (Nos. 188, 189) which was held at the time of the tribal Hunting Dance, and the songs for success in hunting (Nos. 208–217). Both these classes of songs were recorded by Panther, of the Cypress Swamp group. This has not been noted in the dance songs of any other tribe except the Choctaw in Mississippi, the Papago of southern Arizona, and the Makah at Neah Bay, Wash. Such songs were heard at a Choctaw dance and many were recorded (Densmore, 1943 b). The rhythm was indicated by an emphasis on the fundamental tone in a low register. Among the Makah, in similar songs, a man moved his arms during the singing to indicate the time (Densmore, 1939, p. 25). Among the Papago, no accompaniment was used with the songs concerning Elder Brother and his journey, the songs of the tiswin lodge and the wind dance.

Formal and customary endings.—According to Panther, each class of Seminole songs has its own ending which consists of vocalizations after the song. The singers were not encouraged to record the endings with all songs, but a few were recorded and show similarities within groups. The endings are presented with Nos. 2 and 3, which are Buffalo Dance songs, with Nos. 4, 5, 9, and 12, which are Corn Dance songs, and Nos. 100, 101, and 102, which are Stomp Dance songs. In each instance the endings of songs in the same series resemble one another. The transcriptions of many other songs are followed by glissando progressions which may be parts of formal endings or may be a vocalization (cf. Nos. 64, 73, 163, 173, 181, 185, 199, 218, 220, 225, 228). When recording the songs of the Bird Dances, Panther ended the series with sounds that might be called howls or wailing cries, and to these he applied the term "hollering." These were so unusual and interesting that he was asked to record them on a separate cylinder, which he did, showing they could be extended rather indefinitely. Subsequently it was learned this is a custom of the American Negro, described as follows: "The habit of hollering, characteristic of the solitary laborer, has particularly marked the American Negro at work. The holler is a way of singing—free, gliding from a sustained high note down to the lowest register the singer can reach, often ending there in a grunt. It is marked by spontaneous and unpredictable changes in rhythm. In a few instances the glissando progressions precede as well as follow the songs, and occasionally are interpolated in the melody. Such progressions have been noted only at Neah Bay, Wash.

Certain songs were followed by shouts, these being indicated in the transcriptions. As these occur only with certain classes of songs it seems probable they are customary. Such instances are Nos. 75 and 77 of the Baby Alligator and Lizard Dances, Nos. 105 and 106 of the Hinata Dance, and Nos. 190, 191, and 192 of the Crawfish Dance. Two types of shouts were heard and transcribed among the Choctaw, these preceding the Bear Dance and following the Snake Dance. The indeterminate ending and swaying effect of melody and rhythm were also noted among the Choctaw.

Indeterminate ending.—This characteristic of Seminole and Choctaw may be due to the procedure of certain dances in which a song stops when the dancers have completed a circle around the fire. In Nos. 37 and 62 the singer ended abruptly midway through the song and gave the "howls" that follow a completed performance. In Nos. 99, 100, 194, and 195 the transcription ends with "singing continued," as the end of the singing seemed uncertain.   Numerous transcriptions of the songs of Santo Domingo Pueblo are ended in a similar manner.

Ending on tone above keynote.—The first occurrence of this peculiarity was in a dance song of the Cocopa, a Mexican tribe living in southern Arizona (Densmore, 1932 b, p. 182).   Eight songs recorded at Neah Bay have this ending (Densmore, 1939, p. 71), and it occurs in No. 5 of the present series.

Changes of a melody in its repetitions.—This peculiarity is noted in the first period of some songs with period formation, examples being Nos. 11 and 25.   It is possible that more extended performances of other songs with this formation would produce additional examples. In this, as in some other instances, the phonograph cylinder of 2 minutes' duration places a limit of time which would not occur in the Indian's usual performance.   These changes in the repetitions of a phrase suggest improvisation, which appeared to be a custom of the Choctaw and was considered a mark of musical ability by the Tule Indians of Panama.   The custom among the Choctaw was discovered accidentally.   On listening to the recording of certain songs it was noted that the repetitions contained a wide variety of slight changes and embellishments.   The Indian was asked to sing the song again, and he recorded a simple form of the same melody, without embellishments.   This was the song, and the performance was his presentation of it.   Resemblances to the musical customs of the American Negroes have been noted in the music of the Seminole, and it is interesting to note that improvisation is a custom of the Negroes on the Island of Trinidad, in the British West Indies.   According to Louis C. Elson (1880, p. 278) "The power of improvisation so well developed in the African Negro, is fully sustained by his descendants . . ."

"Word swallowing".—This is a peculiar action in which a singer seems to inhale sharply while enunciating a word.   It is described inadequately as "word swallowing" and indicated by × under the note of the song.   This occurred in Nos. 75, 133, 136, 174, 190, and 233.   All were recorded by Billie Stewart, a portion in 1932 and the remainder in 1933.   An additional song recorded by Stewart contained this peculiarity to such a degree that the record could not be transcribed.   It also occurred in one song recorded by Panther that was not transcribed.   When this peculiarity was described to Dr. M. W. Stirling, director of the Bureau of American Ethnology, he stated that he heard it on one occasion among the Jivaro Indians of South America, on his expedition to that country in 1932.

Forcible inhaling of breath.—A peculiar custom of the Seminole is the interruption of a song by a forcible inhalation (cf. p. 162).   This is indicated by × under rests in No. 144.

Only one man sings with a large majority of Seminole dances. The exceptions are the Screech Owl and Snake Dances in which men sing, the Chicken Dance and Cow Creek Hunting Dance in which both men and women sing, and the Cypress Swamp Hunting Dance in which the singer has a "helper." The accompanying instrument is a coconut shell rattle except in the Stomp Dance in which the songs are accompanied by beating on a "cypress knee drum," and the Corn Dance songs in which the accompanying instrument is an ordinary hand drum.

AUTHORITIES CITED

BAILEY, L. H.
 1935. The standard cyclopedia of horticulture. Vol. 2. New York.
BARTRAM, WILLIAM.
 1793. Travels of William Bartram. . . . 520 pp. Dublin.
CULIN, STEWART.
 1907. Games of the North American Indians. 24th Ann. Rep. Bur. Amer.
  Ethnol., 1902–43, pp. 3–846.
DENSMORE, FRANCES.
 1910. Chippewa music. Bur. Amer. Ethnol. Bull. 45.
 1913. Chippewa music—II. Bur. Amer. Ethnol. Bull. 53.
 1918. Teton Sioux music. Bur. Amer. Ethnol Bull. 61.
 1922. Northern Ute music. Bur. Amer. Ethnol. Bull. 75.
 1923. Mandan and Hidatsa music. Bur. Amer. Ethnol. Bull. 80.
 1926. Music of the Tule Indians of Panama. Smithsonian Misc. Coll., vol.
  77, No. 11.
 1928. Uses of plants by the Chippewa Indians. 44th Ann. Rep. Bur. Amer.
  Ethnol., 1926–27, pp. 275–397.
 1929 a. Chippewa customs. Bur. Amer. Ethnol. Bull. 86.
 1929 b. Papago music. Bur. Amer. Ethnol. Bull. 90.
 1929 c. Pawnee music. Bur. Amer. Ethnol. Bull. 93.
 1932 a. Menominee music. Bur. Amer. Ethnol. Bull. 102.
 1932 b. Yuman and Yaqui music. Bur. Amer. Ethnol. Bull. 110.
 1936. Cheyenne and Arapaho music. Southwest Mus. Pap. No. 10. Los
  Angeles.
 1937. The Alabama Indians and their music. In Straight Texas. Publ.
  Texas Folk-Lore Soc., No. 13, pp. 270–293.
 1938. Music of Santo Domingo Pueblo, New Mexico, Southwest Mus. Pap.
  No. 12. Los Angeles.
 1939. Nootka and Quileute music. Bur. Amer. Ethnol. Bull. 124.
 1942. A search for songs among the Chitimacha Indians in Louisiana.
  Bur. Amer. Ethnol. Bull. 133, Anthrop. Pap. No. 19.
 1943 a. Music of the Indians of British Columbia. Bur. Amer. Ethnol. Bull.
  136, Anthrop. Pap. No. 27.
 1943 b. Choctaw music. Bur. Amer. Ethnol. Bull. 136, Anthrop. Pap. No. 28.
 1957. Music of Acoma, Isleta, Cochiti, and Zuñi Pueblos. Bur. Amer. Ethnol.
  Bull. 165. In press.
 MS. Winnebago music. Field Bur. Amer. Ethnol.
ELSON, LOUIS C.
 1880. Curiosities of music. Boston.
ENCYCLOPAEDIA BRITANNICA.
 1937 a. Ginseng. Vol. 10, 14th ed. London.
 1937 b. Nicotiana. Vol. 16, 14th ed. London.
GIFFORD, JOHN C., EDITOR.
 1925. Billy Bowlegs and the Seminole War, with notes and comments by
  John C. Gifford. Coconut Grove, Fla.
HELMHOLTZ, H. L. F.
 1885. The sensations of tone as a physiological basis for the theory of
  music. Trans. by A. J. Ellis. 2d ed. London.

HOMER.
    1932. Odyssey of Homer. Trans. by T. E. Shaw (Col. T. E. Lawrence).
        Oxford University Press. New York.
LEAKE, JAMES MILLER.
    1929. A short history of Florida.
MOONEY, JAMES.
    1900. Myths of the Cherokee. 19th Ann. Rep. Bur. Amer. Ethnol., 1897–98.
        pt. 1, pp. 3–548.
    1907. Calusa. In Handbook of American Indians North of Mexico, Bur.
        Amer. Ethnol. Bull. 30, pt. 1.   Ed., Frederick Webb Hodge.
    1912. Seminole. In Handbook of American Indians North of Mexico, Bur.
        Amer. Ethnol. Bull. 30, pt. 2.   Ed., Frederick Webb Hodge.
MUNROE, RALPH MIDDLETON, and GILPIN, VINCENT.
    1930. The Commodore's story.   [New York.]
NASH, ROY.
    1931. Survey and report made in 1930 to the Commissioner of Indian Af-
        fairs concerning conditions among the Seminole Indians of Florida.
        In U. S. 71st Congress, 3d Sess., Sen. Doc. No. 314.
PEARSON T. GILBERT, EDITOR.
    1936. Birds of America. Pt. 1. Garden City, N. Y.
SADLER, MICHAEL, EDITOR.
    1935. Arts of West Africa. 101 pp. Oxford University Press.
SPECK, FRANK G.
    1911. Ceremonial songs of the Creek and Yuchi Indians. Univ. Pennsyl-
        vania, Mus. Anthrop. Publ., vol. 1, No. 2.
STRACHEY, WILLIAM.
    1849. Historie of travaile into Virginia Britannia. . . . Hakluyt Society.
        London.
SWANTON, JOHN R.
    1922. Early history of the Creek Indians. Bur. Amer. Ethnol. Bull. 73.
    1929. Myths of the Southeastern Indians. Bur. Amer. Ethnol. Bull. 88.
WILLSON, MINNIE MOORE.
    1910. The Seminoles of Florida. New York.
WINTER, NEVIN O.
    1918. Florida, the land of enchantment. . . . Boston.

b, Cory Osceola.

a, Billie Motlo.

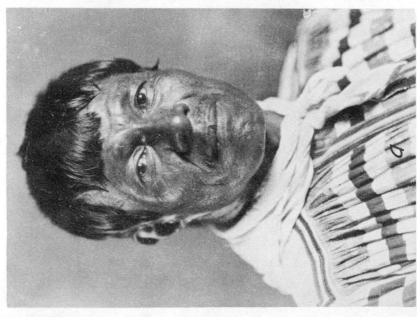

b, Sam Willie and son

a, Tiger Tail.

b, Mrs. John Tiger.

a, Charlie Billie.

c, Billie Stewart.

b, Charlie Snow.

a, Woman drawing water.

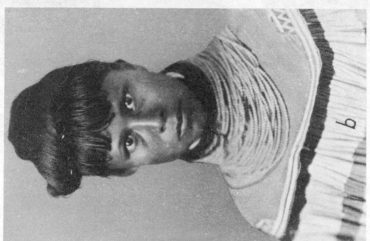

a, Mrs. Tiger Tail.

b, Young woman.

c, Tony Tommie's mother

Seminole scraping a deerhide.

a, Family group.   *b*, Charlie Billie and family.   *c*, Man hewing dugout canoe.

a, Old man in canoe; Chestnut Billie, owner of village, on bridge.   *b*, Seminole poling canoes
in Everglades.   *c*, Cooking in the camp.

a, Seminole at Immokalee. Wilson Cypress making ox yoke. *b*, Scene in temporary camp.
c, Charlie Cypress' hunting camp.

a, Typical Seminole house.   *b*, Seminole women cooking under thatched roof.   *c*, Portion of Musa Isle village in which songs were recorded.

a, Group of Seminole in Musa Isle village.   *b*, View of typical Seminole village from a dirigible. (Photograph by Claude C. Matlack.)   In the village are two enclosed gardens, two rows of houses, and three structures in the center which are cooking or storage structures.   The dock at the left is connected with an open way through the grass of the Everglades.   The dock at the right is connected with slightly deeper water.   The village is on a wooded hammock, and a smaller hammock is seen in the middle distance. This shows the condition in an ordinary season when the villages are reached only by the dugout canoes.

a, Seminole village.   *b*, Typical landscape on southwestern border of Everglades.   *c*, Men poling canoes.

a, Camp in the Everglades.   *b*, Canoe loaded with household goods.   *c*, Boy sailing a canoe.

a, Hides drying on trees; hammock in distance.   *b*, Woman taking washing out of water.
c, Billie Buster's garden.

a, Girls pounding corn.   *b*, Man and woman planting corn.

a, Dance.   *b*, Cooking with typical arrangement of logs.

a, Woman scraping and washing coontie (comtie) roots. *b*, Woman grating coontie roots.
c, Woman stirring coontie flour in barrel.

INDEX

Acoma Indians, 211
Alabama Indians, 171, 172, 198
Alligators, hunted by Indians, 21, 66
Analyses methods, absence of accompaniment, 213–214
  changes of melody in repetitions, 215
  connective phrases, 213
  ending on tone above keynote, 215
  forcible inhaling of breath, 215–216
  formal customary endings, 214
  indeterminate ending, 214–215
  introductory phrases, 212–213
  melodic and rhythmic form, 211
  melodic material, 210–211
  period formations, 211–212
  rise in pitch level, 212
  tone material, 210
  use of the labial m, 213
  "word swallowing," 215
Animal helpers, belief in, 28
Animals hunted, list of, 66
Annie Tommy, informant, xxvii, 21
Arapaho Indians, 198
Assiniboin Indians, 198
Authorities cited, 217–218
Aviles, Don Pedro Menendez de, explorer, 2

Ball, buckskin, 192
Ball game, description of, 192
Ball sticks, used in game, 192
Bananas, coarse, 9, 23
  cultivated, 23
Banding, patchwork, making of, 33
Bartram, quotations from, 40
Baskets, domestic use of, 22
Bathing habits, women's, 20
Bay leaves, ceremonial use of, 34
Beads, worn by children, 16, 20
  worn by women, 19–20
Beadwork, woven, 33–34
Bear, hunted by Indians, 66, 178
Bedding, 15
Belt, panther hide, ceremonial, 42
Betting, habit of Indians, 187
Billie Bowlegs, Cow Creek Interpreter, xxvi, 118, 150, 159, 160
Billie Buster, Indian, 11, 12
Billie Motlo, informant, information from, xxvii, 16, 31, 32, 42, 169, 176, 198
Billie Smith, Medicine Man, 169
Billie Stewart, Cow Creek Seminole, information from, xxvi, xxvii, 11, 12, 28, 38, 39, 53, 56, 60, 65, 70, 71, 81, 86, 107, 110, 117, 119, 129, 132, 134, 141, 144, 147, 159, 162, 169, 186, 187, 192, 196, 200, 215

Blackfoot Indians, 198
Blouse, worn by men, 17
Bobcats, hunted by Indians, 21, 66
Bowdich, T. E., quotation from, 212
Bowles, William Augustus, relations with Indians, 3
Bracelets, silver, 18, 32
Buffalo tail, used by Medicine Men, 186
Burial customs, 34–37
Buttons, silver, 32

Cabbage palm, eaten by Indians, 22
Calendar, compared with white man's, 28
  Seminole, 28
Calusa Hunting Dance, analysis of, 90–91
Calusa Indians, 211
  description of, 59–60, 186
Camp, temporary, 14–15
Canna flaccida, seeds used, 39
Canoe poles, 31, 32
Canoes, 14, 30, 31
  decoration of, 30–31
  making of, 30–32
  models of, 30–32
Capes, worn by women, 18
Charlie Billie, Cypress Swamp Seminole, xxv, xxvii, 40, 41, 66, 85, 155, 156
Charlie Cypress, guide, 7, 8, 10
Charlie Dixie, Seminole Indian, 10, 168
Charlie Snow, informant, xxvii, 70
Charlie Tiger, informant, xxvii, 13, 25
Cherokee Indians, 192, 198
Chestnut Billie, informant, xxvii, 13, 32
Chestnut Billie's Village, life in, 13–14, 16, 20, 22, 26, 28, 32
Children, clothing of, 16
  training of, 27
Chippewa Indians, 156
Choctaw Indians, 65, 107, 192, 211, 213, 214, 215
Clan, Bird, 98
  Panther, xxv, 42
  Turkey, 122
  Wing, 42
Clothing, washing of, 27–28
Clothing and ornaments, 16–20
Coats, worn by men, 42
Cochiti Indians, 211
Coconuts, 25
Cocopa Indians, 156, 215
Cooking utensils, 24
Coontie root, flour from, 22–23
Coppinger's Tropical Village, exhibition village, 15, 27, 120
Córdoba, Fernandez de, relations with Florida, 1
Corn, cultivated, 9, 21
  legend of origin, 197

219

U. S. GOVERNMENT PRINTING OFFICE : 1956 O - 338460